PADDY WALLEY works as a d[...]nd
writer. He graduated in econ[...]n,
studied personal and organis[...]s-
tock Institute, London, and [...]He
works as a consultant to organisations in public, private and community sectors on innovation, human resource and organisational
development. He lectures and conducts seminars in Ireland, USA,
and Europe on a variety of themes in relation to futures including
'The Future of Work' and 'The Information Society'.

He was co-founder and director of the Irish Foundation for
Human Development which did pioneering work on personal,
organisational and social development. He has conducted development programmes with company managers and community lead-
ers for the International Fund for Ireland; he designed and directed
a European Commission Pilot Project on Education for Development.

His writings include *Learning the Future*, a book on education
for the Knowledge Society; research reports for public, private,
community sectors; contributed to the Thomas Davis Lectures
Series 'The Jobs Crisis' and also 'The Future of Work'; articles in
national newspapers. He has contributed to radio and television
programmes on work and the knowledge society, and related
themes.

OLIVER DONOHOE is a Social Science graduate of University College,
Dublin, whose experience includes development work in Nigeria
and Mauritius and researching for the Late Late Show in RTE
where he also produced features and current affairs programmes.
He conducted a wide variety of education and training courses for
the Irish Congress of Trade Unions from 1975 until 1987, when he
became Congress' Research and Information Officer, with responsibility for monitoring economic and social change and developing
media relations and communications.

He has written several articles and papers on a range of socio-
economic topics and is currently editor of *Network News*, the news-
letter of Congress Unemployed Centres, and of *Construction Today*,
a publication for the building industry.

He is a member of the National Council for Curriculum and
Assessment and of the NCCA's Working Group on the new Leaving Cert Ap[...]

He is [...] undation's co-
ordinating g[...] the Public Services and A[...] of Congress on

What we are experiencing is not a crisis of modernity.
We are experiencing the need to modernise the pre-
suppositions upon which modernity is based.

ANDRE GORTZ

IRELAND
IN THE
21ST CENTURY

PADDY WALLEY

Edited by
OLIVER DONOHOE

MERCIER PRESS

MERCIER PRESS
PO Box 5, 5 French Church Street, Cork
16 Hume Street, Dublin 1

© Paddy Walley & Irish Congress of Trade Unions

ISBN 1 85635 120 3

10 9 8 7 6 5 4 3 2 1

A CIP record for this book is available from the British Library.

Printed in Ireland by Colour Books Ltd.

CONTENTS

FOREWORD

I am excited by this unique book and pleased to be involved in its publication. It grew out of a debate which took place at a Conference on 'Ireland in the 21st Century' organised as part of Congress' centenary celebrations. The Conference brought together a distinguished panel of national and international contributors.

This book recognises the progress which has been made in the past century and points to new challenges for the future. It highlights the increased importance which learning and innovation will play in our lives and the need to shape the changes which will impact on all of us in the next century.

This book does not lay down the law. It lays out options and choices we have to make individually and collectively. While some recommendations are made and preferences indicated, the emphasis is on description rather than prescription.

It is refreshing to read a book about the next century which is based on the premise that we have the capacity to shape our own future. *Ireland in the 21st Century* gets the balance right in its account of the threats and opportunities presented by the technological revolution, the global economy and the knowledge society.

The forces of change are nowhere more clearly in evidence than in their sweeping and profound effect on the world of work. This book pulls no punches in its description of what the new century holds in store for organisations or societies that do not equip themselves with the new knowledge, insight and skills required by an innovative society.

Because each piece of the change jigsaw is put in context, the full picture takes shape as we read. Like a new 3D puzzle, when we look closely at the picture, we see that the focal point is the person at the heart of change. Recognising that change is not neutral, this book underlines the importance of subjecting the forces for change to the influence of human values.

In recognising the importance of being open to change, it also recognises that not all change is necessarily good. There are many important values and structures in our culture which need to be maintained and nurtured. For example, if part-time and temporary employment is not to become a means of exploiting the vulnerable, the values of justice and fairness will have to be built into the contract of employment.

There are also recent developments in social solidarity and human rights which need to be extended and consolidated. For example, the right of people with a disability to be employed in paid jobs in the open labour market should not be diminished by high levels of unemployment.

Ireland in the 21st Century spells out the opportunities and challenges that affect all of us. They are exciting challenges with the potential to improve the quality of our lives. The only thing as certain as change itself is that this book will change the way we look at the future. Enjoy it.

PETER CASSELLS
IRISH CONGRESS OF TRADE UNIONS
JUNE 1995

INTRODUCTION

In looking towards the 21st century, we can see that there are powerful forces of change at work which are transforming society. This process is changing the types of jobs, the pattern of production and the means of creating employment. Tremendous opportunities for creating new employment and improving living standards are emerging as the global economy is projected to grow strongly into the 21st century.

It is also a time of great danger as communities and countries face being marginalised and left behind. People's skills and organisations' development strategies need to be upgraded continuously to ensure that they participate effectively in the expanding knowledge based, global economy.

In commenting on this transition, the EU White Paper on *Growth, Competitiveness and Employment* points out:

> this decade is witnessing a forging of a link of unprecedented magnitude and significance between the technological innovation process and economic and social organisation. Countless innovations are combining to bring about a major upheaval in the organisation of activities and relationships within society. Throughout the world, production systems, methods of organising work and consumption patterns are undergoing changes which will have long term effects comparable with the first industrial revolution.

This book aims to identify some of the important issues involved in this transition and their implications for Ireland, as we approach the 21st century. It is intended, not as a blueprint, but as a help to understanding some of the changes affecting our lives and, particularly, the world of work.

THE FORCES
OF
CHANGE

The forces which are causing the transformation in the Irish
and global economy and society are a combination of
Changing Values and Lifestyles, New Technologies,
Globalisation and other Workplace innovations.

VALUES AND CHANGE

In recognising the importance of being open to change, it is also important to be aware that not all change is necessarily good, and that change is not a neutral process. Values must be applied in all relationships to change. There are many important values and structures which represent vital aspects of human culture that need to be protected in the process of change — for example, access to satisfying work opportunities for men and women, the issues of social justice and equitable distribution of wealth, care of the old, the sick, the vulnerable, care for the environment, a spirit of conviviality, community and interpersonal solidarity, a right to diversity, difference and dissent, and openness of decision-making. All of these values need ongoing nurturing in the face of individual and collective aggression, tendencies of dominance, uniformity and injustice, which are strong forces in society.

CHAPTER 1

VALUES AND LIFESTYLES – PEOPLE ARE CHANGING

Changes in values and lifestyles are important dynamics of change in the economy and society, bringing demands for new types of products and services, and changes in the nature and organisation of work. A significant cause of unemployment has been the failure of businesses in Ireland to identify the new trends in values and lifestyles, and create products and services to meet them. Failure to shift to new areas of demand results in the decline of business and job losses.

The structure and nature of many aspects of European and Irish society have undergone profound change in the past twenty years. Many of the products and services on offer and many aspects of Government and social policy lag far behind these changes in people's values, attitudes and perceived needs.

1 – People are Better Off

The majority of us in Ireland and Europe are much better off in terms of housing, diet, education, health care and incomes than we were 50 years ago. Increased wealth, which has come with growth in the economy and wages, means we have more money available to spend on other goods, in addition to food and shelter. We are also more discriminating about the quality and the value of the goods and services we purchase. This affluence is predicted to increase significantly into the 21st century. Income per head in Europe and Ireland is projected to grow by 30% over the next 15 years.

This growth in affluence and concern with quality and uniqueness is changing the type of products and the quality of services being offered. It has also dramatically reduced the lifespan of products as people's tastes change frequently and more people can afford to indulge these changes by buying new goods or services. This is changing the world of work as organisations and businesses respond to these evolving patterns.

Business is now being structured to become more customer friendly and responsive to changing consumption patterns. Products and services are being upgraded continuously and new ones are being offered. This is resulting in a wider variety and more niche focus in the goods and services produced. There is a growing emphasis on excellence and customers' rights in both the creation and delivery of products and services. Everyone providing services will need to be responsive to the rising expectations of customers in relation to quality and value.

2 – People are More Individualised
People are more individualised than in the past. Individuals are becoming more proactive and discriminating in defining their own needs and in managing their own lives. The increased range of options available to people in their work and leisure opportunities has resulted in the emergence of a wider concept of personal development than heretofore. The expansion in options is leading to more diverse and complex patterns of living. For many people, this wider opportunity and responsibility for choice of living patterns is liberating and enriching.

However, the wider world of choices means that people are not just given wider options but are confronted with the compulsion to choose in a complexity of options which many find confusing, isolating and overwhelming. The sense of security of identity and of belonging, which was given by a world of more proscribed and limited options, is being replaced by a much more insecure, uncertain and isolated sense of self. There has been a weakening of the power of many of the traditional structures which defined social reality and gave access to strong identity – the church, employing organisations, class, traditional family and nationality. These were the traditional forms of social cohesion and collective belonging. Identity is now created more through individual creativity than through the taking up of traditional roles which were firmly defined.

These constructed realities are much more insecure and vulnerable than realities based on inherited collective structures. Individuals and groups are in danger of being isolated from each others' realities with the resultant loss of social cohesion. Creating social cohesion in this more individuated and diverse world will require a more active commitment among people to inter-personal solidarity, as new forms of social bonding will be needed. New forms of social cohesion will need to combine support for the emerging individual desire for diversity with opportunities for accessing a sense of belonging in ways which do not demand conformity and sameness.

This wider concept of individuation is a significant cultural change, which has deep implications for Irish society in the 21st century. While individuals want more personal autonomy and responsibility, they also need the experience of belonging and fear the insecurity of the compulsion of choice and rapid change in the social environment. In the face of this fear, they can easily retreat into self-contained realities of extreme individualism and social disconnectedness on the one side, or group fundamentalism on the other.

In Ireland, we have been, in many ways, a very traditional culture. We have maintained closed and traditional structures, which did not promote individual choice and diversity. Belonging and conforming went close together in providing security of identity. Adapting to the society of diversities and personal choice will be a fundamental social challenge and will involve a lot of learning at all levels of our culture.

Fortunately, our membership of the EU has begun to integrate us into the broad stream of a diverse European culture, which strikes a good balance between these extremes of individualism and group fundamentalism. Creating collective structures which do not demand conformity, but promote and support individuals' differences and diversity, will be one of the significant challenges of the 21st century. It will require profound individual and social learning to create unity based on diversity.

Phil Flynn, President, ICTU, speaking at the Congress Centenary Conference in Dublin Castle, said:

> The main purpose of our collective action is to enhance the lives of the individual women and men who give us our collective strength. Our ability to meet that challenge may well be the major determinant of our relevance to the needs of working people in the 21st century.

3 – Attitudes to Work Changing

The rising levels of education and affluence are resulting in changes in people's attitudes to work. People are increasingly concerned about the quality of their working lives. In addition to its monetary rewards, people have higher expectations in relation to finding workplaces which offer personal autonomy and challenging opportunities for creating. Other expectations include whether one's employability for the future is enhanced by the quality of the work, educational opportunities, and the network of relationships to which it gives access. People also expect work to be a place where one is treated with respect and is a fulfilling part of life. These attitudinal changes will bring pressures for redesigning and upgrading workplaces in a society where skilled, well-motivated people will be much sought after.

Surveys carried out by the public opinion Institute in Germany, Allensbrach, show that the perception of life as a task and social duty has diminished, whereas the perception of life as pleasure has increased considerably, particularly among under 30s.

Life as Work versus Life as Enjoyment

	1960	1964	1973	1977	1980	1982	1990
	% Share of Total Population						
Life as Task	60	59	48	48	51	43	18
Enjoying Life	29	29	35	38	29	36	39

Source: Societies in Transition: The Future of Work and Leisure, OECD, 1994.

4 – Leisure More Important

The amount of discretionary, non-job related time in our lives has expanded enormously in the past 50 years. The result is that leisure or non-work activities have become a more significant part of our lives than in the past. Leisure activities are a growing part of people's identities. Leisure activities are also becoming a major source of demand for new products and services and new sources of employment.

Examples include: sport, fitness, music, learning, travelling.

The extension in the amount of non-work time in people's lives has come from the combination of the following:

a) decline in the length of working life due to:

(i) the much later entry of people into the workforce; less than 25% in most developed countries start work before they are 18 years old

(ii) the length of the working year has declined from 3,500 hours in 1920 to 2,050 hours today in Japan, 1,866 in Ireland, 1,800 in USA, and 1,500 in Germany. The decline in the number of hours worked is projected to continue. This reduction in working time is a goal of development in a number of countries – Japan aims to drop from its current level of 2,052 to 1,806 by the year 2010; Norway from 1,400 to 1,300 in 2010.

Average hours actually worked per person per year

	1970	1973	1975	1979	1983	1990	1991	1992
Total employment								
Canada	1890	1865	1837	1794	1730	1733	1713	1709
Finland	1982	1915	1885	1859	1798	1756	1758	1728
France	1962	1904	1865	1813	1711	1669	1667	1666
Italy	1969	1885	1841	1788	1764	–	–	–
Japan	–	2185	2100	2110	2081	2023	–	–
Norway	1766	1694	1653	1501	1471	1415	1408	1417
Spain	–	–	–	2148	2052	1941	1931	1191
Sweden	1641	1557	1516	1451	1453	1480	1468	1485
United States	1886	1875	1833	1808	1788	1782	1771	1769
Dependent employment								
France	1821	1771	1720	1667	1558	1539	1540	1542
Germany	1885	1804	1737	1699	1670	1573	1557	–
Netherlands	–	–	–	1591	1530	1433	1423	–
Spain	–	–	–	2032	1947	1858	1847	1828
United States	1836	1831	1791	1767	1754	1749	1737	1736

Source: Employment Outlook, OECD, 1993, p. 186.

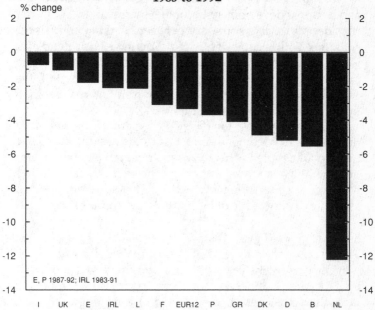

Change in hours worked per week in the member states, 1983 to 1992

% change

E, P 1987-92; IRL 1983-91

I   UK   E   IRL   L   F   EUR12   P   GR   DK   D   B   NL

Source: Employment in Europe, European Commission [Employment, Industrial Relations and Social Affairs] 1994, p. 103.

b) Longer Life

In addition to the shortening of the job life, the increasing longevity of people has expanded the free time which people have. People now live considerably longer lives than in the past. The average lifespan in EU countries has increased by 10 years in the past 40 years.

In the EU, reducing the working week further is seen as a means of sharing work and reducing unemployment. The general rising prosperity makes this more feasible as more people can access high living standards in shorter working time. Modest projections for economic growth show a 25–30% increase in real incomes for those in employment over the next fifteen years.

23

Rising prosperity is bringing a shift in values in relation to work and non-working time activities, with quality of life and personal development becoming increasingly significant considerations. The boundary between working and leisure activities will become less rigidly defined with people at work having more personal responsibility for the planning of work, more sense of enjoyment and fulfilment within the culture of work and more satisfaction from internal competitiveness and group co-operation.

Preparing people for the management of discretionary time needs to become an important part of education. The capacity of people to effectively and qualitatively use leisure time will have a strong impact on the effect these activities will have in generating new employment and wealth, as well as on the quality of life of individuals and communities.

5 – Educational Levels Rising

The educational threshold of people globally has risen significantly in recent years. World adult literacy is estimated by the United Nations to have increased from 15% in 1953 to more than 60% in 1993. The number of technologically literate people is growing rapidly. There are now 600 million technologically literate workers in the world able to operate complex manufacturing equipment. In the next 20 years, this figure is expected to rise to 3 billion. Governments everywhere are increasing their expenditure on education and training, as there is a clear correlation between educational capacities and economic growth. The OECD *Jobs Study* points out that 'productivity and income levels are highly correlated with levels of educational attainment and professional skills'.

People are becoming more aware of the growing importance of education for employment. Those with the lowest educational levels have the highest levels of unemployment, as there is a continuing decline in numbers of unskilled jobs. This is resulting in increasing enrolment of young people beyond compulsory education in Ireland and most OECD countries. At present 73% of those who enter second level education in Ireland complete the senior cycle. The policy target for the Irish Government is that, by the year 2000, 90% of the age group would complete the senior cycle.

Enrolment rates of young people at age 17 and 18, 1991
Enrolments as a percentage of all persons in corresponding age group

AT AGE 17		AT AGE 18	
Greater than 80%		**Greater than 70%**	
Japan	88.8	Germany	80.0
Belgium	88.1	Switzerland	75.9
Sweden	85.3	France	75.0
Finland	85.2	Norway	74.8
Norway	84.7	Finland	73.4
France	83.3	Netherlands	72.7
Switzerland	82.0		
Germany	81.6		
Between 70%–80%		**Between 50%–70%**	
Canada	79.3	Denmark	67.6
United States	77.0	Canada	59.2
Netherlands	73.6	Sweden	55.7
Denmark	73.3	United States	55.0
Ireland	70.6	Spain	52.0
		Ireland	**50.1**
Less than 70%		**Less than 50%**	
Spain	64.3	Portugal	42.0
New Zealand	58.9	New Zealand	32.7
Portugal	49.0	United Kingdom	25.7
United Kingdom	44.3	Turkey	24.6
Turkey	31.9		

Source: The OECD Jobs Study, Evidence and Explanations, Part II, The Adjustment Potential of the Labour Market, 1994, p. 130.

There is still considerable room and urgent need for improvement as the employment prospects for early school leavers will be very poor in the future. In the emerging knowledge society, the large percentage of young people who leave school without higher level qualifications face very poor job prospects. For society, it is a serious social problem being created for the future as the diagram on page 26 shows. About 22% of those at work in Ireland in 1990 had no qualifications while this was true of over 40% of the unemployed. Three-quarters of those unemployed had either no qualification or an Intermediate or Group Certificate.

25

Employment Status by Level of Education of those in the Labour Force, Aged 15–24 Years 1990

Level of Education	At Work	Unemployed	Total	Percentage Unemployed
		Number		%
No qualifications	15,800	13,500	29,300	46.1
Inter/Group Cert	73,100	26,600	99,700	26.7
Leaving Cert	111,100	14,300	125,400	11.4
Third-Level	36,200	3,000	39,200	7.7
Not Stated	500	200	700	28.6
Total	236,600	57,600	294,200	19.6

Source: A Strategy for Competitiveness, Growth and Employment, NESC, 1993, p. 481.

Participation rates in full-time education for various age groups

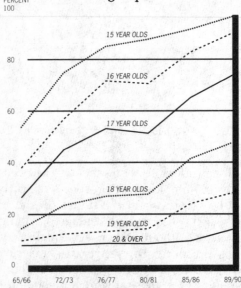

Note: the participation rate for 20 years and over is estimated on the basis of the 20–24 age cohort of total population.

Source: Irish Department of Education, Green Paper, 1994, Statistical Appendix.

Full-time education enrolment rates for persons aged 17, 18 and 22

	17 YEAR-OLDS					18 YEAR-OLDS					22 YEAR-OLDS			
	1985	1989	1990	1991	1992	1985	1989	1990	1991	1992	1985	1989	1990	1991
Australia	–	73	77	80	–	–	47	48	52	–	–	–	–	7
Austria	–	–	–	–	86	–	–	–	–	–	–	13	14	14
Belgium	82	80	81	85	–	64	54	57	73	–	13	19	21	18
Canada	78	78	78	81	–	55	66	68	58	–	15	27	28	22
Denmark	81	–	83	79	–	66	–	71	69	–	24	–	34	29
Finland	85	88	89	85	–	66	72	75	72	–	30	–	34	35
France	81	86	89	90	90	58	70	71	78	79	14	17	20	21
Germany	96	–	100	93	95	82	–	91	81	84	26	28	35	36
Greece	–	58	65	–	–	–	35	36	–	–	–	–	25	–
Ireland	**66**	**72**	**73**	**76**	**90**	**40**	**47**	**50**	**51**	**–**	**–**	**9**	**9**	**9**
Japan	–	88	89	89	–	–	–	–	–	–	–	–	–	–
Netherlands	79	85	87	87	–	68	70	71	74	–	19	22	24	26
New Zealand	35	53	55	60	–	19	29	31	34	–	6	9	9	11
Norway	75	76	82	84	87	60	61	72	75	78	22	20	27	29
Portugal	37	60	–	59	–	34	47	–	45	–	14	–	–	11
Spain	51	60	62	64	–	38	47	50	52	–	20	24	27	27
Sweden	82	86	85	85	87	47	51	52	56	61	15	17	17	18
Switzerland	83	85	86	86	85	74	77	77	77	77	15	16	17	17
Turkey	–	23	24	26	–	–	17	18	19	–	–	6	6	7
United Kingdom	31	36	41	43	–	18	20	23	25	–	–	6	6	7
United States	88	84	83	80	–	53	54	54	55	–	15	16	18	18

Source: Employment Outlook, OECD, 1994. p. 28.

New forms of learning

New forms of learning opportunities need to be developed through which all young people can achieve success in areas where they have competence. This success provides a base for lifelong learning. The new Leaving Certificate Applied is an important development in this area. The old model based on a once-off 'win/lose' ethos with built in failure is not suitable for a learning society and creates a base of failure for too many people in relation to learning. A deeper awareness of the importance of education needs to be actively promoted throughout society.

Education in work is also increasing as the knowledge content of work is continuously being updated and the products and services change frequently. People are also investing more time and resources privately in learning for reasons of personal development in a wider sense than the purely economic. As people become more affluent they can attend to broader aspects of self development than simply economic or survival needs. The growing importance of education is likely to continue. Learning will become a major activity throughout life and a central part of the workplace in the 21st century.

6 – Population Structure Changing

(i) Birth Rate Decline

There has been a dramatic decrease in the birth rate in Ireland and in the EU since the 1960s (see the diagram on next page). Ireland's birthrate is now 13.7 per 1,000 – the EU average is 11.6 per 1,000. To maintain a country's overall population needs a replacement rate of approximately 2.1 children per woman – Italy is now 1.5, Spain 2.9, and Ireland 1.93. This decline will also result in an ageing workforce and a population with different tastes and needs than a society dominated by younger people. It will also result in a decline in the proportion of people of working age in the population.

(ii) Life Span Increasing

As well as a decline in the birth rate, there has been a dra-

Birth Rate per 1000 in Ireland

Source: 'Labour Market Outlook and the Structure of Employment in Ireland in 1978' by John Fitzgerald and Gerard Hughes in Labour Market Review, Volume 5, No. 1, FÁS, Winter 1994, p. 32.

matic increase in the life span of people. Due to improvements in diet, housing, medicine, especially pre-natal care, and general life style, people are now living much longer. The number of people who are older in Ireland and other OECD countries will rise significantly in the years ahead. In 1990, those over 60 totalled 100 million in OECD. The number is expected to rise to 130 million by the year 2010 and 156 million by 2020 (see diagram on next page).

Ratio of Workers Declining
The share of the population of working age will steadily decline so that the older age dependency ratio will increase from 19% in 1990 to 28% in 2010 to 37% in 2020; Japan and Germany will have an age/dependency ratio of 34% by 2010. The overall average number of 'workers' per elderly person in Europe has declined from about 7.5% in 1960 to about 5.4% today and projected to drop to about 2.5% by 2040. Pensions, health and social services will be supported by only one-third of the employment base in 2040 compared to 1960. In addition to the growth in people over 65 years, there is also the build-up in numbers of frail people who are elderly

(over 80) and need intensive care services. This means an increase in productivity will be needed to maintain and develop social services.

Age Dependency Ratio

Persons 65+ as % of persons aged 15–64

	1990	2040
Belgium	21.9	41.5
Denmark	22.2	43.4
Germany	23.7	47.1
Greece	20.5	41.7
Spain	17.0	41.7
France	21.9	39.2
Ireland	18.4	27.2
Italy	20.4	48.4
Luxembourg	20.4	41.2
Netherlands	17.4	48.5
Portugal	16.4	38.9
UK	23.5	39.1
EU	21.4	42.8

Source: Federal Trust, USA.

While the growth in people who are older will bring an increased need for care, this will also be a very significant source of new employment and of demand for new products and services. Many people who are older will have considerable purchasing power due to accumulated pensions, savings and properties. There will also be a large number of people who are older and dependent on State pensions for survival, and on public services for health care, home help and intensive nursing. These numbers will continue to grow. It is one of the characteristics of any society claiming to be civilised, that people who are older are assured of financial security, medical services and caring support to live comfortably and, where possible, independently. Planning for our ageing population must become an integral part of planning for the 21st century.

Due to improved health and working conditions many people in their 60s, 70s and 80s are now very active and productive. The continuation of this pattern will bring a fundamental change in our view of ageing and retirement. Many people are sufficiently healthy and active to begin new careers on retirement from their 'first' career. New patterns of employment may be needed to tap into the knowledge and skills of people who are older. New leisure activities and educational opportunities will also be needed by these people, who see themselves as capable of active enjoyment of life and as resources rather than a burden on the community.

7 – Workforce Ageing

The decline in fertility rates will result in the shortage of workers becoming a major issue in the EU and industrialised countries generally in the 21st century. There will be considerable skills shortages in many areas of the European economy. For Irish people, this will be very good news. To meet these opportunities, we will need to ensure that everyone in our society is given opportunities to upgrade their skills and encouraged to appreciate the importance of education and training. Since increasingly the workforce in work will also be the workforce of the future, continuous education of those in work will be essential.

The ageing of the workforce will also transform the demands on our educational system. The demand for education and training will grow as workers will need continuous re-learning and people who are older will have time and resources for learning. Much of our leisure activities will involve learning. Education will expand from focusing on the business of preparing young people for work and life, to include the production of focused learning products for already well educated adults. Higher education and 'leisure' learning skills for recreational activities will also expand to meet the growing demand.

8 – Environmental Awareness Growing

People are increasingly seeing the natural and built environment as a significant part of the quality of their lives. This heightened awareness of the environment is coming from growing leisure time and affluence, which gives people the

31

opportunity to enjoy the environment. There is widespread concern about the damage of pollutants to people's health and the growing evidence of environmental damage caused by our lifestyles and systems of producing food and manufactured products. These concerns are changing people's lifestyles, methods of production, technologies and sources of employment.

The restoration of urban centres is now a significant source of employment. Eighty percent of the population of the EU live in urban areas. This urbanisation process is likely to grow in the 21st century.

People are increasingly discriminating in relation to the health and environmental effects of products, which is resulting in industries seeing 'environmental friendliness' as an important part of their competitive advantage. Education and travel focused on understanding and enjoying the environment are now major service industries. Many see environmental awareness as being a central dynamic in shaping lifestyles and employment in the 21st century.

9 – Health Improving

There is a growing appreciation by people that their health is affected by their lifestyles and the quality of life of their society. It is not simply a gift of the gods. The result is that people are actively managing their health through diet, exercise and relaxation and they are more conscious of the effects of the quality of their relationships on their general well-being. The growth in marriage separation is, in some ways, an expression of this awareness that unhappy or unfulfilling relationships are bad for one's health and that good relationships are good for one's health.

This awareness of the importance of conviviality and of the quality of relationships will also affect the organisation of work. There is growing evidence that environments pervaded by fear and lack of joy are not good for productivity and may be a cause of illness.

Food and the quality of air are beginning to be recognised as being linked with cancers. There is also evidence suggesting that a diet of bad relationships and emotions can also be contributory causes of cancer. The ability to manage stress is now becoming an important life skill.

Growth in health awareness can have significant effects on the capacity of the economy to grow, and therefore on the overall wealth of a society. With healthier living, resources that would be wasted on illnesses (which people would not get with better lifestyles) can be devoted to positive investment in education, leisure facilities, culture, technological infrastructures, and research. These investments enhance the capacity of society to create and generate wealth and employment. People's health improves primarily through changing behaviour.

An important component of economic development for the future will be, not just the productivity of people in work, but the whole quality and efficiency of people's lifestyles. This will be particularly true as people spend more of their lives outside the workplace.

10 – Family Structures Changing

The traditional assumptions of industrial society about the structure of the family and the participation of men and women in the workplace have been bypassed by changes in society, which are profoundly altering both the structure of the family and the participation of men and women in paid employment.

The traditional family of industrial society was composed of mother, father, children, with father going out to paid employment and mother looking after the children. This is no longer the reality for most families.

The breakdown of marriage is now a common feature of life in Europe, resulting in a growing pattern of serial monogamy, with people separating and forming new partnerships. As people live longer, divorce is doing for some relationships what death did previously. Marriage for life meant 15–20 years in the past, now many people form partnerships for different purposes at different stages of much longer lives. One in three marriages in Europe now ends in divorce. Cohabitation without marriage is common, and increasingly it is becoming socially accepted. A growing proportion of children are being raised in single parent families. In Denmark, the UK, and Germany, one household in ten with a child under the age of 10 is a one-parent family and in some parts of the USA it is as high as 1 in 4.

The result is that a new concept and experience of the extended family is developing for some, in which one has step-partnerships and new uncles and aunts, not necessarily blood related, and new stepbrothers and stepsisters. The society now emerging is being marked by a variety, flexibility and diversity in family life similar to the variety beginning to emerge in the organisation of work. The traditional industrial model of the nuclear family is now being seen as one kind of family structure. The 'merged' family is a concept used to describe another kind of family structure.

11 – More Women, Less Men in Paid Employment

The participation of women and men in the paid workforce is changing. This seems to be driven by (a) changes in the nature of the work becoming available, with a growth in work that is less muscle intensive and more service-based, (b) the changing structure of the family, and (c) changing values, particularly among women. The participation of women in paid employment is growing in all European countries, and that of men is declining. In Ireland in 1994, 41% of women were in the labour force.

While participation by women in Ireland in paid employment has grown in recent years, it is still the lowest in OECD countries, as can be seen from the illustration on page 36. Denmark and Sweden have the highest participation rates in Europe, with 80% of women in paid employment. While the number of women in paid employment has increased throughout the EU, the number of men has declined. This is particularly the case for men over 55. The decline in male employment seems to be a reflection of the disappearance of blue collar work and to a lesser degree, middle management. It is also a reflection of a decline in the number of young males in the labour force as they stay in school longer than in the past.

Male/Female participation in paid employment

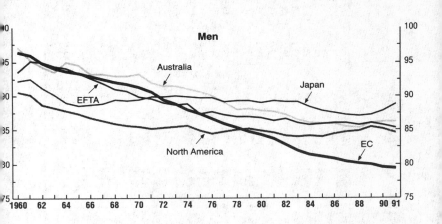

Men

Australia

Japan

EFTA

North America

EC

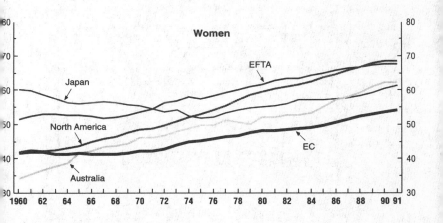

Women

EFTA

Japan

North America

EC

Australia

Source: The OECD Jobs Study, Facts Analysis Strategies, OECD, 1994, p. 16.

Labour force participation rates by sex (percentages)

	Men						Women					
	1973	1979	1983	1990	1991	1992	1973	1979	1983	1990	1991	1992
Australia	91.1	87.6	85.9	85.9	85.6	85.3	47.7	50.3	52.1	62.1	62.2	62.4
Austria	83.0	81.6	82.2	80.1	80.5	81.3	48.5	49.1	49.7	55.4	56.3	58.3
Belgium	83.2	79.3	76.8	72.7	72.8	–	41.3	46.3	48.7	52.4	53.2	–
Canada	86.1	86.3	84.7	84.9	83.9	83.4	47.2	55.5	60.0	68.1	68.1	67.9
Denmark	89.6	89.6	87.6	89.6	88.5	–	61.6	69.9	74.2	78.4	78.9	–
Finland	80.0	82.2	82.0	80.6	79.6	78.5	63.6	68.9	72.7	72.9	71.8	70.6
France	85.2	82.6	78.4	74.6	74.5	–	50.1	54.2	54.4	56.1	56.8	–
Germany	89.6	84.9	82.6	80.8	80.6	80.1	50.3	52.2	52.5	57.0	58.1	59.0
Greece	83.3	79.0	80.0	82.1	–	–	32.2	32.8	40.4	39.9	–	–
Ireland	**92.3**	**88.7**	**87.1**	**82.2**	**81.9**	–	**34.1**	**35.2**	**37.8**	**38.8**	**39.9**	–
Italy	85.1	82.6	80.7	78.9	79.4	79.2	33.7	3.7	40.3	44.9	45.8	46.3
Japan	90.1	89.2	89.1	87.8	88.9	89.3	54.0	54.7	57.2	60.4	61.5	61.7
Luxembourg	93.1	88.9	85.1	–	77.7	–	35.9	39.8	41.7	–	44.8	–
Netherlands	85.1	79.0	77.3	79.9	80.3	–	29.2	33.4	40.3	53.0	54.5	–
New Zealand	89.2	87.3	84.7	82.2	82.3	–	39.2	45.0	45.7	62.4	62.8	–
Norway	86.5	89.2	87.2	84.5	82.9	83.0	50.6	61.7	65.5	71.2	71.1	70.9
Portugal	100.8	90.9	87.6	86.1	85.9	–	32.1	57.3	57.2	60.4	62.8	–
Spain	92.9	83.1	80.2	76.8	76.0	74.9	33.4	32.6	33.2	40.9	41.2	42.1
Sweden	88.1	87.9	85.9	85.3	84.5	82.7	62.6	72.8	76.6	81.1	80.3	78.7
Switzerland	10.6	94.6	93.5	96.2	95.3	–	54.1	53.0	55.2	59.6	59.8	–
UK	93.0	90.5	87.5	86.5	86.1	85.6	53.2	58.0	57.2	65.3	64.5	64.5
United States	86.2	85.7	84.6	85.8	84.7	85.0	51.1	58.9	61.8	68.6	68.4	68.9
North America	86.2	85.8	84.6	85.7	84.6	84.8	50.7	58.6	61.6	68.5	68.4	68.8
OECD Europe	88.7	84.8	82.3	80.6	78.3	–	44.7	48.6	49.8	54.8	54.0	–
Total OECD	88.2	85.9	84.3	83.7	82.4	–	48.3	53.1	55.1	60.7	60.5	–

Source: Employment Outlook, OECD, July 1993, p. 192.

The extent of the change in male/female participation can be seen clearly in the period 1965–1990, when the number of women in paid employment grew from 39 million to 54 million, while the number of men decreased from 83 million to 82 million. Of the 10 million new jobs created in the period 1985–1989 in the EC, 30% went to men, 70% to women. The rising participation of women in paid employment and the relative decline in male participation is likely to be one of the most important formative trends in the world of work of the 21st century.

Changes in total employment of men and women in the Member States, 1985–89

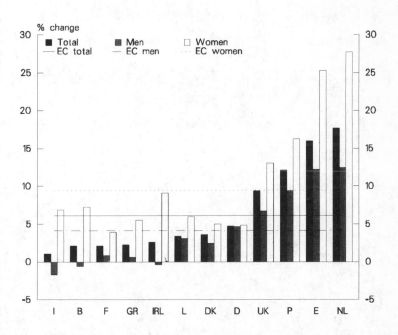

Source: Employment in Europe, Commission of European Communities [Employment, Industrial Relations and Social Affairs], 1991, p. 24.

CHAPTER 2

TECHNOLOGY AND CHANGE – THE NEW REVOLUTION

The world is undergoing a major technological revolution. A core of new technologies is replacing the technologies which formed the basis of 'industrial' society. This will fundamentally alter the nature of work and the structure of Irish society in the 21st century. When the technological structure changes, the infrastructure of society changes. Dr Cornell, Deputy Secretary of the OECD, describes the depth of technological change as follows:

> I think that we are beginning to see that the entire world, especially the industrial countries, are going through a period of immense and very disruptive wrenching technological change. Not technological progress which we all have learned to live with since the beginning of this century or at least since the end of the World War II but technological change probably in its disruptive effects of the order of the impact of electricity or, before that, steam propulsion. If we look back in history these major technological changes produced major upheavals in the economies that experienced them, but at the end of the day things were better than at the beginning. The problem was, getting over the change, altering institutions and ways of behaviour, ways of doing business and ways that adapted to the change even as the winners turned out to be those economies, those societies that accepted the change more rapidly than others did.

Mr Phil Flynn, President, ICTU, commenting on the extent of the technological revolution, stated:

> The 'technological revolution' may be close to becoming a cliché, but this concrete reality is well illustrated by the estimate that the developed world currently possesses the technological capacity to eliminate half of the new existing jobs and by the unveiling recently of the Digital Corporation's latest computer chip which can process more than one billion instructions a second. Our greatest challenge is to ensure that such magnificent achievements of human kind are used to improve not worsen the quality of life of working people.

The new technologies include:

1) Information and Communications Technologies
2) Bio Technology
3) ECO Technologies
4) Space Technology

5) Energy Technology
6) New Materials Technologies

The development and application of these technologies will alter society more fundamentally than did the industrial revolution. Organisations and societies which are successful in applying the new technologies will prosper. Those who fail to do so will be marginalised and decline as they waste resources trying to maintain and reproduce the past.

These technologies are resulting in a virtual explosion of new knowledge, of products, of ways of organising and of meeting human needs. The most significant of these is information technology as it underlies and pervades all aspects of the economy and enables the building of a global economy organised around information.

1 – Information and Communications Technology

The core technology of the emerging knowledge based economy is the computer and the information and communications technologies which have resulted from its invention. Information and communications technologies are seen as the backbone of a new economy. Information and communications technologies are huge industries in their own right. Producing the machines (hardware) and the programmes (software) is the fastest growing sector of manufacturing industry. More significantly, information and communications technologies are enabling technologies which provide the infrastructure for a deep transformation of the whole economy and the world of work.

Information technology in the narrow sense refers to the computer, which is a machine invented for the automatic processing of information. It is regarded as a radical innovation in the development of technology, which has the potential to fundamentally change the nature and organisation of work in society even more than did the steam engine and electricity.

The first electronic computer (ENIAC) was built in 1946, weighed 30 tons, contained 18000 vacuum tubes. Now the same computing power is contained in a single silicone chip.

41

Any home computer could now out perform the ENIAC in processing ability. The computer chip is now part of most electronic products, from washing machines, to cars, TVs, and telephones. Penetration by the chip is becoming so pervasive that the term 'smart products' is now being used. There is an explosion in the variety of new types of computers with a diversity of uses in business, entertainment, health and transportation. Virtually every aspect of life will be affected by the impact of these technologies.

Communications technology includes television, satellites, cables, telephones, and faxes. Recent advances in methods for inter-linking computers and these technologies enables the instant transportation of voice, texts and images, to virtually anywhere in the world. What comprises information and communication technology is continuously broadening as these technologies are rapidly evolving. They cover an exploding range of products which are expanding their influence daily on the shape of work, the economy and culture generally.

The creation of local, national and global 'information highways' is now considered central to development strategies in every country. Companies, communities and countries that are not linked into these networks risk marginalisation and exclusion from the next stages of economic and social development. Internet is the most famous of these. These networks are called 'Information Highways' and are seen as the nervous system of the 21st century economy which will be created around information.

Information and communications technologies expand the capacity of society to use information more extensively in all aspects of life. The different elements of these technologies, (computers, telephones, TV, etc.) are now being combined to enable the linking of more activities directly together. Video conferencing, shopping via TV and hundreds of TV stations are all part of the emerging menu. These changes are transforming the nature of products through the expansion of their knowledge content. They are also transforming the whole organisation of work. By reducing time and distance to zero, time and distance are no longer obstacles to the organisation of work. Once the infrastructure is in place, it is now possible to have instant inter-connection of people and places, through data and images, anywhere in the world.

Information and communications technologies facilitate much more rapid responsiveness in organisations to people's needs as instantaneous information feedback is possible. Extensive automation of production with 'intelligent' machines is now possible, as is the development of distance medical diagnosis and treatment through transmission of images across unlimited distances. The design of products in simulated realities and the redefinition of education and learning through the use of these technologies are now also possible. The global inter-connection between schools and other centres of learning and information opens great possibilities for international learning co-operation between young people, as well as enhanced opportunities for open learning. Virtual realities also open new possibilities for training in simulated realities.

Information technologies have opened new doors for advances across all the areas of scientific knowledge, e.g., biotechnology, genetic engineering, environmental services and space technology. Information technology enables biotechnology to create extensive international research projects into the structure of DNA, diseases and new plants, therapies and medicines. The results of this research are likely to have dramatic effects on our understanding of many diseases, of the process of ageing, on the production of new plants and on agricultural and industrial products and productivity.

Dr Eamon Hall told the Congress Centenary Conference about the effects of information technology on work:

> The effects of information technology on work – at the factory level – range from the automated inventory to computer-aided manufacturing and robotisation resulting in the increase of process efficiency. Obviously, this will result in increased speed of production, customisation, communication. By involving employees in general business and services analysing, synthesising and making decisions on the data, employers can improve the effectiveness of all in the process by discovering new and better ways of doing work. Shoshana Zuboff, an expert in information technology, calls this process the use of in-

43

formation technology to 'informate' employees rather than 'automate' them. This is the challenge facing us. We do not want the new technology simply to speed up business practices and reduce staff. Attention must be focused on the relationship between people and process; employee consultation and training must not be an afterthought.

The global organisation of work is now possible – a new global integration of manufacturing is being created, using these technologies. Global financial markets which the new technologies have enabled are now a formative force in the world economy. A wide range of new products for working and leisure activities in the home is also being created. Making these technologies is a huge industry which the EU estimates will be worth 2,000 billion ECUs by the year 2000. Information and communications technology contribute about 5% of world GDP and 8% of GDP of industrial countries and is growing faster than any sector.

2 – Biotechnology – Genetic Breakthrough

Biotechnology has emerged from the breakthrough made by science in understanding the genetic code of plants, animals and humans. Biotechnology is the process of creating and applying the knowledge of biology. Its application covers a broad spectrum of life from food production and medicine, to the environment. It provides a wide range of new products and services and creates employment in agriculture, health care and environmental management. It is forecast by some commentators as the primary technology of the 21st century.

Biotechnology includes activities like fermentation and brewing, selective breeding of plants and animals, genetic engineering, gene therapy and pollution control. It has enormous potential for improving the environment, identifying the basis of illness and preventing and treating disease.

The capacity of science to explore the inner workings of the cellular life of plants and animals and the ability to intervene in this process has been greatly expanded by information and communications technology. Information technology enables vastly more complex computations than were previously possible. A particularly interesting example of biotechnology in the field of genetics is the recent international research project called the 'Human Genome' project which aims to decipher the code in the human gene.

The sectors of employment which are affected by biotechnology include chemicals, pharmaceuticals, health care, agriculture, food processing, and waste treatment. It is estimated that sectors which biotechnology affect account for 9% of the EU value added (450 billion ECU) and 8% (9 million) of its employment. Global prospects for biotechnology can be seen in these figures – the USA had a turnover of 8 billion in 1992, a growth rate of 28% in output, and 13% growth in employment. It is estimated that biotechnology sales will grow at 40% per annum to reach 52 billion by the year 2000. In Japan, present value is 3.8 billion and estimated to reach 35 billion by the year 2000; EU biotechnology is estimated at 3 billion. By the year 2000 the world market of biotechnology is projected to be 100 billion. It is seen as an important source of new high value, high skilled employment in chemicals, pharmaceuticals, agriculture and food, research, health care and environmental management.

In agriculture, biotechnology is seen as having huge potential to raise productivity and output and help prevent world food shortages. Through the increased output it makes possible, it will reduce further the employment needs in farming, e.g., growth hormone will double the cow-output of milk, which means fewer dairy farmers. Bio-technology will alter the food output in farms but can also create synthetic food products in laboratories. Potentially crops can be developed and produced indoors similar to other manufactured products. This may change the nature of food production into one integrated process, from DNA through production to marketing, all taking place within integrated food companies, with the disappearance of traditional agriculture.

Dr Dave McConnell, in his paper to the Centenary Conference, outlined developments in genetics and biotechnology:

As geneticists world-wide are starting on the Human Genome Project, 'one of mankind's greatest odysseys' (Sir Walter Bod-

45

mer), the new genetics revolution is affecting all fields of biology, from medicine and agriculture to aqua culture and biotechnology.

The Human Genome Project will decode the complete genetic blueprint, that is the complete DNA sequence of the million or so human genes which programme the human being. Along the way there have already been striking genetic discoveries, for example in medical genetics and the genetics of cancer. There are more than 5000 different genetic diseases and about one child in 50 is born with a significant genetic disease, for example, haemophilia. Asthma, allergies, diabetes, vascular disease, cancer and many other diseases are caused by a combination of genetic and environmental factors. Already, about 100 genes have been identified which are related to cancer, including some which have been strongly implicated in breast cancer. We are able to prevent many genetic diseases, such as cystic fibrosis, fragile X, muscular dystrophy, haemophilia, etc. and in some cases, advise about risks of cancers. Professor Peter Humphries in my department is one of the world's experts in the genetics of blindness and his work is opening up exciting but speculative ideas about applying gene therapy to the eye ....

... Genes are also being used to develop new medical procedures. The DNA sequence data are pouring in to computerised databases in Los Alamos and in Heidelberg – so far 200 million pieces of data are in and this will rise to 400 million in 18 months from now and 800 million in 36 months. The Irish National Centre for Bioinformatics (NCBI) housed in Trinity College also holds the DNA sequence database, and it is frequently updated from Los Alamos. The total human DNA sequence is 3 billion units (A, T, C and G) and we would hope to have that completely decoded in 10 to 20 years. These data will be used by the pharmaceutical industry to build new drugs of many different kinds and there will be parallel advances in many aspects of agriculture and other biological sciences, using the knowledge of DNA sequences. We will be able to read the blueprint of the cow, rice, the salmon, yeast and so forth, and therefore we will be able to design knowledge-based ways of improving the different organisms.

... Genetics is, of course, only one science among so many that are going to influence our society profoundly in the 21st century. I have tried to give some feeling for what it has to offer, but other sciences will have their own surprises.

3 – ECO Technologies – For a Better Enviornment

The increasing affluence and leisure in people's lives in developed economies has brought a growing awareness of the environment as a resource. This includes both the natural and the built environment. Since 80% of Europeans live in urban areas, the quality of the built environment is an important issue in determining the quality of life. There is also a growing anxiety about the implications for the health and survival of the human species arising from the build up of pollution from many of our working and living practices.

The combination of these concerns is resulting in the creation of a whole new set of technologies called 'eco technologies'. They are 'technical innovations targeting the causes of pollution and aiming at environmental efficiency through the production cycle'. Eco technologies are being seen as a source of major competitive advantage as environmental awareness grows. They are also seen as significant sources of new wealth and employment. These technologies range from research equipment and systems for understanding the functioning of the natural environment to technologies for improving urban water and sewage systems. They include renewable heating systems and production technologies needing lower energy and raw material inputs.

The EU *White Paper on Employment* proposes the creation of a model of economic development which will be more environmentally friendly – 'sustainable development'. It sees the environment as a significant new source of jobs and wealth creation.

4 – Space Technology – Down to Earth
Space exploration and space research is an ongoing and significant area of research. This research on materials, technologies and life in gravity free environments is providing advances in knowledge and in engineering and life sciences which will have practical effects in everyday life. It is also providing opportunities for growing international co-operation. A number of large, new national and international projects are under way or being planned in the USA, the EU, Japan, China, and Russia; e.g., the USA has a $30 billion project to create a permanent orbiting science research institute, and the EU is planning to build a European staffed space vehicle. The USA and Russia have signed a $400 million contract to support a joint research programme. Recently, the first Japanese woman took part in an international space

shuttle. Twenty commercial satellites are launched each year. France controls 50% of this activity. This is likely to grow rapidly as communications become an increasingly significant aspect of economic and social activity.

The use of space as a focus for research is likely to continue to expand. Exploring space is still a project which has tremendous fascination for people, and its continued expansion in the next century is likely to impact profoundly on day-to-day life on this planet.

5 – Energy Technologies – More Power, Less Pollution

Since World War II there has been a vast expansion in energy consumption to support the rapid growth of the world economy. World energy consumption increased by an average of 5% per annum, from 1950 to 1973, twice the rate of the nineteenth century. It is estimated that society globally will have used as much energy in the second half of the twentieth century as throughout the whole of human history prior to 1950. From 1970–1992 energy consumption grew at 2% per annum.

Since 1950 the structure of sources of energy has changed fundamentally with the large scale replacement of solid fuels (particularly coal, by oil and, more recently, gas and nuclear power). In 1950 oil accounted for 10% of Europe's energy requirements, and increased its share to 53% in 1970. It now accounts for 45%, solid fuels still account for 21% and nuclear power has grown from 4% in 1970 to 14%, while gas has increased to 18%.

Primary Energy Consumption by Fuel (%)

	Coal	Peat	Oil	Gas	Nuclear	Other
Ireland	22.4	13.2	48.3	15.4	0.0	0.7
EC	21.0	0.0	44.8	18.3	14.3	1.6

The data for Ireland are for 1991; the data for the EC are for 1989.

Source: Issues in Irish Energy Policy, edited by John FitzGerald and Daniel McCoy, ESRI, Paper No. 20, December 1933, p. 20.

Ireland's sources of energy are similar to the rest of the EU with one distinction, that Ireland has no nuclear power and peat (15%) plays the same role as nuclear power does in the European average. Some European countries have extensive nuclear programmes, e.g., France generates 78% of electricity needs through nuclear power. Nuclear power energy grew rapidly in the 1980s as it was seen as a secure and non-polluting source of energy. However, it has not grown in the 1990s due to the fears provoked by Three Mile Island and Chernobyl. Consumption of energy is almost evenly divided between three main sectors – industry (31%), transport (31%), household and tertiary sector (38%) with household alone covering 27%.

The combination of the oil crisis in the 1970s and the increasing concern about damage to the ozone and global warming caused by the build up of 'Greenhouse' gases, has resulted in considerable expansion in research into new energy technologies. This is directed to developing new sources of energy, to reducing the polluting effects of energy use and the energy intensity of the economy. A range of research programmes on energy technologies, focused on both the production and consumption sides, is being undertaken internationally. These range from nuclear fusion to technologies which use biomass, wind and solar power.

On the consumption side technological research is focusing on reducing the polluting effects of transport (particularly the motor car), of industrial methods and the heat use of buildings. In many countries legislation is bringing stricter controls and forcing technological innovation. International competition is also bringing pressures to reduce energy costs, both to the economies and the environment.

6 – New Materials – Endless List
The materials which form the basis of the products and services in modern economies are in a continuous process of evolution as new research, knowledge and people's tastes are incorporated in their creation. Upgrading the materials base is an essential part of upgrading the quality of the economy. New materials form the base of many product innovations and are a significant aspect of competitive advantage. For example, advanced composite materials have

transformed the aerospace industry and are now transforming the design of major components for automotive, medical, maritime and leisure applications. They have a range of benefits over steel and alloys – greater fatigue resistance, reduced weight, increased stiffness and reduced tooling costs.

Ongoing investment in new materials is extensive – for example Bayer in Germany invested over 60 million DM in 1992 developing new plastics, rubber, polyurethanes, coating materials and silicones. These materials are increasingly being used in the automotive, construction, electrical and electronic industries to improve product design and performance, to develop better foams to insulate buildings and to make vehicles lighter and more energy efficient.

Advances in new materials have lead to the development of new techniques which enable the coating of components in industry with harder coating which results in increases in the operational life of parts and components in machines.

CHAPTER 3

GLOBALISATION – A NEW WORLD EMERGING

The growing inter-connectiveness of societies and the economies of the world is likely to be a central feature of the 21st century in its effects on cultures, trade, work and the organisation of society, including the role of the nation state.

Globalisation is a term used to cover a number of trends in world development:
(i) The increasing integration of the economies and cultures of the world;
(ii) The growing size and power of multinational companies;
(iii) The rising economic capacity of the economies of developing countries.

1 – Development on a Global Scale

The process of global economic development is a dynamic process of leap-frogging with countries changing the products they produce and the technologies they use, as they improve their levels of skills, technologies, wages and living standards. This process of leap-frogging can be seen very dramatically in Asia. The increasing sophistication of the economies of Singapore, Taiwan, and Korea is resulting in labour intensive industries moving to the lower waged, lower skilled countries of China, Indonesia, Vietnam, etc., which are more recent entrants into the global economy.

This process of leap-frogging is promoted by Governments actively discouraging low skilled investment – for example, the Singapore Government raised wages as a strategy to upgrade the jobs and investment it was attracting. Singapore is very similar to Ireland in its heavy dependence on multinational investment. Singapore, Korea, and Taiwan are growing so strongly that the average income is predicted to be higher than the USA in 10 years. This growing capacity of developing economies can be seen in the changing composition of world output and trade.

2 – Information Village – Diversity or Uniformity

As the information and communication technologies are becoming more integrated globally, and more comprehensive in their representational capacities, there is a growing flood of information and images across national boundaries and continents. People everywhere can now have almost instant access to information on events happening anywhere in the world. A virtual information village is being created. This open flow of information brings new opportunities and problems in relation to culture and identity.

On the positive side, it enables people all over the world the opportunity to share, enjoy and learn from the diversity of ways of living practised around the world. It also makes it more difficult for people to be isolated and oppressed by closed societies, as it is almost impossible for Governments to block access by citizens to the external world. The collapse of the Communist regimes in Eastern Europe was finally precipitated by the open access to the world which the fax, the telephone, radio and TV provided for the people of Eastern Europe.

On the negative side, this open flow of information and the growing role in people's lives of TV, videos, and films, is causing concern about the tendency to cultural uniformity. The USA, for example, controls 80% of the output of the audio/visual industry. It raises questions about how nations can influence the values and images which these media bring into people's homes. How can society internationally ensure the continued existence of the diversity of each of the cultures which enriches the human experience? Can the global inter-connectiveness be managed to improve the sharing of this diversity? To what extent can we allow the 'market' to be the arbiter of what is good or right in human values?

3 – Money Makes the World Go Around
The global flow of information is seen very dramatically in the huge growth in the international financial markets. There is now a 24–hour continuous global flow of financial trading amounting to a thousand billion dollars per day which is 160 times the size of world trade in goods. These financial dealings have major consequences for Government decision-making and the competitiveness of companies and countries. Many Governments are virtually powerless in the face of

these forces as the experience of attempts to establish an EU single currency demonstrates. A major political issue will be the creation of political mechanisms which will give Governments more control over these financial markets.

The movement of finance has become so significant that changes in currency values can be the primary force in defining the cost competitiveness of countries and companies. A fluctuation in currency can be more important in determining companies' cost competitiveness than labour costs. This global money market and currency speculation will be a significant political issue in the 21st century.

4 – Global Companies – Co-operation or Domination

The combination of information and communications technologies with organisational innovations has resulted in the emergence of global companies which organise their production within a global structure. In these global organisations different aspects of their production of products can be located in different parts of the globe. A global web of adding value is a good image of the structure of these companies, where different parts of the value adding process are carried out in different countries or continents. The location of activities is defined by the comparative advantages which different countries have over others.

It is increasingly difficult to say where any product is made, as they are composites of activities performed in different countries.

For countries like Ireland, which uses multinationals as a significant source of employment, the part of this 'value adding web' which is located in this country can be very important in determining the type of jobs available here. It is in the high value adding parts that the high wage, less footloose jobs are located. In the low adding value, repetitive work, the low waged, more footloose jobs are located.

The power of these global companies is very considerable and growing.

- One-third of world output is controlled by multinationals;

- One-third of world trade is within multinationals – up from one-fifth in the early 1970s;
- One-fifth of non-farm jobs in industrialised countries are supplied by multinationals;
- 10% of non-farm jobs world-wide are provided by multinationals.

Peter Sutherland, Director General, GATT, told the Congress Centenary Conference:

> One result of globalisation has been the consolidation of a large share of private economic activity in many countries around enterprises that have an international dimension. Estimates indicate that multinationals directly employ 20% of the (non-farm) labour force in OECD countries, and the percentage is likely to be much higher in small trade-dependent countries such as Ireland. This trend poses challenges to the traditional relationship between Governments and enterprises, and between trade unions and employers.

The concentration of trade, employment and investment in multinational corporations is affecting the power of even large Governments to control their economies. Decisions on investment location by multinationals can dramatically alter the fate of communities. The movement of plants to avail of the different competitive advantages of the different countries is made easier by globalisation. This has increased the competition between countries in relation to multinational employment. Governments are played off against each other by these companies, as they pursue higher grants and better tax concessions. The threat of relocation, whether real or not, can alter the balance in favour of employers in their negotiations.

This competition is particularly strong in relation to labour intensive, low skilled employment, such as routine assembly work or data processing. Globalisation has given easy access to vastly increased numbers of low waged labour for repetitive work. This part of the global value adding chain is much more footloose than work which has high skill content. Rather than looking for unskilled jobs for unskilled workers, development strategies should focus primarily on upgrading the skills of the workforce and thereby upgrade the quality of jobs which can be accessed. Ireland has one of the highest dependencies on multinationals for employment in the world, and the highest in Europe. This could mean that a slight shift in multinational investment patterns globally could have very significant repercussions on employment in Ireland.

5 – Globalisation and World Trade
(i) Output Boom
Since World War II, the economies of the world grew more than in all human history before that with an accompanying growth in living standards in most countries. That growth was driven by the expansion of trade. As the ILO points out in its report *World Employment:*

> World output has grown by at least 3% per annum since 1960. Between 1966–1973 growth rates were close to 5% per annum before slowing to 3.5% 1970–1980 and 1.1% in 1990s, largely due to recession in industrial countries. Global output is now projected to return to the 3% range which prevailed since 1974. These growth rates have exceeded population growth, yielding a steady increase in per capita output. In 1990 total world output in real terms was almost double what it had been in 1970 and real per capita output was around 26% higher. From this viewpoint, that is if we abstract from problems of distribution within and between countries, it is apparent that there has been considerable global economic progress. This progress has been driven by increased world trade.

(ii) Trade without Frontiers
The increasing integration of the economies of the world is resulting from a combination of a) political change in Eastern Europe and China, b) the revolution in information and communication technology, c) the GATT agreement, d) declining transport costs, and e) new forms of work organisation. The combination of these developments is resulting in a much more open flow of investment, goods, services and technology around the world. Labour is the factor which has the least mobility. It is predicted that world trade will grow rapidly into the 21st century.

Peter Sutherland, Director General of GATT, predicts a growth of $500 billion annually will result from the GATT agreement. This growth will benefit most countries in the world, but with particularly strong growth in East Asia. Parts of Africa are in danger of being marginalised and disconnected from this new global economy. Peter Sutherland said:

> The economic benefits of the Round are enormous. Literally incalculable, since reliable estimates for services trade are not available. But the limited estimates we do have put the extra world income at around $500 billion annually by 2002. For Ireland, the Fitzpatrick report has indicated an overwhelmingly positive result, one that is already being felt in improved confidence and investment and growth as the more cheerful international outlook bolsters European recovery.

Within this overall expansion there will be large increases in trade within northern economies and also in certain types of north/south trade. The growth in emerging economies offers tremendous potential for Ireland and other European economies in the increased demand for infrastructure, consumer products, and services. The growth in east Asia is predicted to be 6–7% per annum in comparison to 2.5% for Europe and the USA. In talking about 2.5% of the economies of Europe or the USA, one is not talking about 2.5% increase from zero, but of truly enormous economies.

China is growing at a rate of 10% and, with 1.5 billion people, is predicted, as Minister Ruairi Quinn pointed out at the Centenary Conference, to be the biggest economy in the world by the year 2000. This rapid growth in the emerging economies may result in EU share of world trade declining. In considering the likely change in the share of global trade, it is interesting to look at the position of EU in world trade at present. With just 7% of the working population of the world, EU produces and consumes 25% of world GDP. According to projections by Cooper and Lybrand (UK) based on growth in EU of 2.5%, and Asia of 6% per annum, western Europe's share of world trade will fall from 25% to 18% by the year 2010, while Asian countries' share will rise from 18% to 28%. This change in the distribution of world trade does not mean a decline in European living standards or the size of European trade, as one is not talking about a share of a fixed amount, but of a much larger global economy.

(iii) Structure of World Output

Share in world trade percentage, developed and developing world

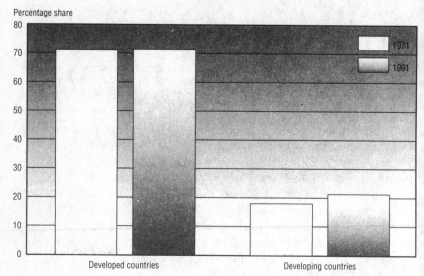

Source: World Employment 1995, An ILO Report, 1995, p. 32.

Since 1960 there has been a considerable shift in world output from agriculture to industries and services. In 1960, 10% of world output was agriculture and it is now 4%. Manufacturing has increased considerably in developing countries where its share of output is now 20% which is similar to developed economies.

iv) Distribution of Trade

While world output and trade have grown strongly and developing countries have rapidly industrialised since 1960, the relative share of world trade between developed and developing economies has remained the same. The gains in developing countries in growth and capacity were primarily in east and south-east Asia, with relative stagnation or decline in Africa, and slow improvement in South America.

Manufactures as a percentage of total exports, 1970–90

	1970	1980	1990
World	60.9	64.2	71.1
Developed countries	72.0	70.9	78.0
Eastern Europe	59.1	50.2	43.9
Developing countries	18.5	18.5	53.9
Asia	28.4	23.5	65.5
South and south-east Asia	43.4	51.0	77.7
Latin America	10.6	14.7	30.8
Africa	7.0	4.0	15.1

Source: World Employment 1995, An ILO Report, 1995, p. 33.

(v) Composition of Trade

Where previously the trade between developing and developed economies consisted of the south sending raw materials north and the north sending manufactured goods south, trade from the south now primarily consists of manufactured goods. These goods are still mainly labour intensive manufactured products, like textiles, clothing and footwear, while exports from the north have a high skill content. However, the Asian countries have increased their market share in the knowledge intensive sector, such as office equipment, electronics and telecommunications. The annual sale of southern manufactured goods to the north has grown from nil in 1950 to 250 billion in 1990, growing at average rate of 12%. While it is a large figure, it still is only 3% of the imports of developed economies.

6 – The World at Work

To represent the growth in trade with developing economies

as the cause of unemployment in developed economies is to misinterpret reality. Up until now, the figure has been too small a percentage of trade in developed economies to have caused the high growth in unemployment. The OECD *Jobs Study* points out:

> most of the competition in OECD countries, which includes Ireland, comes, not from low wage countries, but from OECD countries themselves. For the most part, trade between OECD countries involves trade within sectors, or even within firms, involving the exchange of intrinsically similar products with broadly similar labour and skill contents. Globalisation is further strengthening the growth of this kind of trade, making the trade between OECD countries more and more like trade within OECD countries. Analysis of trade in goods suggests that there has been a small negative effect on demand for unskilled labour in OECD countries, due to trade with non-OECD countries, but that losses of unskilled jobs have been largely offset by jobs gained through trade in goods produced by skilled labour.

The study by Nguyen, Perroni and Wigle takes a long-term perspective on long-term sectoral adjustments in employment in the north and south predicted from GATT as the table on page 61 points out. The most prominent changes are in agricultural and the light industry sector dominated by textiles and clothing. Employment in agriculture is predicted to fall by between 10% and 20% in the industrialised world. Employment in light industry will fall by over 20% in Europe and 35% in North America. The employment increases in the north in the services sector are small in percentage terms but are among the largest increases in absolute terms. The 1.9% increase in employment in the European Community's service sector is as large in absolute terms as the predicted employment loss in EC agriculture of 14%.

Some commentators point out that the fear of developing economies' capacity to take traditional markets rather than the reality has resulted in job losses, as companies have automated labour intensive production in anticipation of competition from low cost countries. However, as the OECD points out, the vast bulk of job losses in the 1980s in developed economies came from obsolescence in products and technologies, failure to create new products and services

Sectoral employment changes in North and South (resulting from implemementing the Uruguay Round)

	Agriculture	Intermediates (Basic)	Mining	Light industries	Forestry & fishing	Capital goods	High tech. manufacturing	Intermediate (manufacturing)	Services
North									
United States	-10.1	-0.3	1.2	-36.0	-0.4	3.0	4.5	1.1	0.5
Canada	-11.6	0.7	2.4	-33.3	0.2	3.2	4.0	1.2	0.7
EC	-14.0	0.9	-0.4	-23.6	1.0	3.9	12.2	2.4	1.9
Japan	-21.5	1.9	-3.2	-13.5	-1.6	2.8	3.6	2.5	0.8
Australia & New Zealand	3.6	-1.2	3.7	-28.4	0.4	-2.8	-1.3	-1.0	0.7
Other North	-14.3	1.3	-0.4	-22.7	0.9	4.2	14.9	1.8	1.4
South									
Industralising agri-cultural exporters	-2.5	-0.6	-0.6	5.6	-0.2	-2.2	-4.3	-1.0	0.4
Industralising agri-cultural importers	-16.6	2.9	-5.8	82.8	-4.3	-7.0	-7.8	-5.3	-2.7
Centrally planned	0.7	-0.2	0.2	4.4	0.2	-3.5	-2.4	-1.2	-0.7
Others	0.8	-1.4	2.1	8.5	-0.2	2.0	-2.4	-1.0	-0.3

Source: World Employment 1995, An ILO Report, 1995, p. 39.

and failure to innovate. Trade from developing countries is a tiny fraction of trade in developed countries.

> Imports from low-wage countries are not primarily importantly responsible for today's unemployment. Let us take just a brief glance at the evidence. Trade with non-OECD countries represents less than 5% of GDP in North America and Western Europe, meaning that competition from low-wage countries is not a significant factor in OECD countries. Furthermore, non-OECD countries are good customers; they buy at least the same amount of exports as OECD countries combined from North America and Western Europe, demonstrating that trade with low-wage countries is 'win-win'. And countries with the highest rates of import expansion in recent years – Korea, Thailand, Hong Kong, China, Mexico, Costa Rica, Chile among others – have consistently recorded low or declining unemployment rates. So imports do not lead to unemployment ...
>
> (PETER SUTHERLAND, GATT)

However, in the next century, this competition from developing countries for investment in these countries, and for markets in developed economies for both low and high tech products, will grow. This increased capacity of developing economies should be welcomed for the improvement in standards of living it brings to these countries and also for the innovative pressure it puts on business and society in developed economies. It also brings cheaper products for consumers in developed economies. This growing capacity of developing economies is intensifying the pressures for economic change all over the world, improving economic growth, technological innovation, literacy levels and living standards As Michael Hansenne, Director, ILO, said:

> First, rapid technological progress and the intensification of economic globalisation have led to increased interdependence of the world's labour markets. Not only have closer ties emerged among labour markets in the industrialised world, but also between industrialised and those of some developing countries.
>
> A number of developing countries moving towards industrialisation have switched their main export activity from primary products to manufactured projects, particularly those using relatively low-level technologies. This has led to new patterns of industrial production and a changing international division of labour. Western industrialised countries no longer have that clear advantage in exporting manufactured goods, and developing countries exports are no longer concentrated

only in primary commodities. All this has meant that, while in the past, large gaps in real wage levels, particularly for low-skilled workers, did not pose any real threat to low-skilled manufacturing sector jobs in the industrialised world, they do so today. Globalisation of the economy imposes adjustments on the part of both industrialised and developing countries.

7 – Work without Walls

The result of this growing capacity of developing countries has brought calls for protectionism from some people in Ireland, on the basis that it is unfair competition as these countries' costs are much lower. Protectionism would reduce the opportunities for these countries to develop and result in loss of trade and new jobs in Ireland which their development potentially can create. It would also remove a valuable pressure for innovation on industries in developed economies. The response to these advances of developing economies cannot lie in protectionism or slowing the process of change. The only suitable response in developed countries is to innovate into new, higher level activities. Labour intensive, low skill industries, which are the industries most directly threatened by low cost structures of developing countries, do not represent the industries which form the core of a modern economy.

In commenting on protectionism, Peter Sutherland said:

Protectionism is sometimes presented to workers as an attractive option. You only have to look at the evidence of the last hundred years to see how wrong this is – protectionist responses made the Great Depression of the 1930s a disaster for working people around the world and hastened the slide into war. If protectionism is an option, it is the suicide option.

Robert Cornell, OECD, commented:

Of course, an option for a nation as a whole, an economy as a whole, is to try to insulate itself from what is going on in the rest of the world, this globalisation process, this technological change. Most countries are opting not to do that because they realise that to cut oneself from what is going to be viewed a decade from now as an immense wave of progress is going to ensure that economy, that society, that country is one of the losers rather than one of the winners through this whole process. On the other hand, the problem is that just to remain non-protectionist does not guarantee that you are going to be a winner. It only guarantees that you have a possibility of being a winner if you have the right structural policies and macro-economic policies to go along with, if your strategy, in other words, is correctly chosen. At the end of the day it is going to be those strategy choices by societies, by Governments, by employers and by the Social Partners that will decide whether or not countries are winners in the global game that is now under way.

8 – Is Ireland Vulnerable?

While the growing markets of developing countries offer tremendous opportunities for Irish business, they also present challenges for Ireland, due to the following:

a) multinationals account for such a large amount of employment;
b) so much of Irish indigenous industry is in the low skill, older products category which are most vulnerable to competition from developing countries;
c) we are a small economy.

What would be a tiny shift as a percentage of overall multinational investment could be a major dislocation for employment in Ireland. This consideration should be carefully built into future strategy on multinational investment. Particular concern has been expressed about relocation in Eastern Europe, which has a skilled workforce and a long industrial tradition, particularly in engineering, and is located close to the centre of Europe. In future, routine data processing work will be in direct competition with countries such as India, who have huge numbers of computer skilled people with wage levels that are minimal compared to Ireland.

9 – Has the Nation State a Future?

The growing integration of the EU, the increasing power of multinationals, and globalisation of communications and financial flows are eroding many of the traditional powers of the nation state. Simultaneously, the traditional power of the nation state is being weakened from the other end by the growth in the power of more localised development structures. These developments are resulting in new questions about the future role and influence of national Governments.

Robert Reich, US Minister for Labour, in his book *The Work of Nations* argues that 'the idea of a national economy has become meaningless as is the notion of national corporation, national capital, national products and national technology'. He feels that Governments' concern for making companies profitable, or getting good returns for investors is not appropriate as, in a global economy, companies and investors move easily around the world wherever they can make money – they have no nationality. The only legitimate role for Government in relation to employment is to enhance the skills of the people, to improve their ability to add value in the global economy.

Michael Porter, of Harvard, argues that the national Government has become more important than in the past, but in new ways. In a world in which the traditional idea of a static inherited comparative advantage of a country is being replaced by an active one of competitive advantage, based on created factors, Governments have the central role in creating the factors which give countries competitive advantage. These factors are different for different countries and are continuously changing.

In examining the effects of globalisation on the nation state, Dr Rory O'Donnell, National Economic and Social Council, pointed out that the changes in economic and social life have altered the process of Government decision-making. He pointed to two particular changes, 'the increase in the role of regional and local Government in economic management' and 'the move to greater collaboration between the State, State agencies and organisations which represent the interests of those most affected by policy'. This he saw as a shift from the State as decisive in policy-making and implementation to the State as a partner in economic and social governance with groups such as the social partners:

> As I have emphasised, Government remains critical in achieving successful economic and social performance. But this critical role depends less on what the state does itself, than on the way in which it co-ordinates, prompts and facilitates action by a range of state agencies, mandated agencies, interest groups, company networks and voluntary associations.

In addition to its critical role in relation to employment, active Government policies are also critically important in relation to the provision of health, education, welfare, environmental protection and macro-economic budgetary and taxation policies. Different strategies by different Governments greatly affect the functioning of societies.

Professor Galbraith feels that there will be ongoing tension between the thrust towards globalisation, towards larger economic and political union and the continuing power and relevance of national Governments. He sees this dialectic as one of the areas of primary social tension in the future.

While there has been a growth in the power of supra-national institutions, there has also paradoxically been a growth in the power of institutions smaller than the nation state; regions, cities and local communities have become much more active in taking responsibility for their development, either directly or in partnership with public and private institutions. International networks between cities and regions are now part of the development landscape. The Italian industrial districts are internationally famous as models of local development success; local systems of innovation involving collaboration between colleges, business, trade unions, voluntary groups have achieved prominence in literature on development.

In Ireland there is now an extensive network of local development structures. Decentralisation, subsidiarity and devolution of decision-making are now seen as an integral part of how a modern society functions. Local development is also seen as a way of integrating the enterprise of people more directly in decision-making, of deepening the democratic process and as a new dynamic for job creation.

10 – World Working Conditions

There are many people who are concerned that low labour and environmental standards are giving some developing countries low cost advantages. There are also objections that trade with these countries should be conditional on raising labour and environmental standards. The argument is that by allowing this trade we are supporting repressive regimes, labour exploitation and environmental destruction.

The International Confederation of Free Trade Unions which represents 120 million workers world-wide has actively sought the linking of the observance of basic internationally recognised workers' rights to international trade. The ICFTU proposes that a clause along the lines of the following should be included in the GATT and similar international agreements:

> The contracting parties agree to take steps to ensure the observance of the minimum labour standards specified by an advisory committee to be established by the GATT and the ILO, and including those on freedom of association and the right to collective bargaining, the minimum age for employment, discrimination, equal remuneration and forced labour.

It argues that:

> Universal adherence to the seven basic standards would prevent the most extreme forms of exploitation and cut-throat competition. It would not end developing countries' comparative advantages but establish a process by which labour conditions could gradually be improved as trade increases, in particular through focusing attention on productivity improvement. This would encourage the growth of consumer markets thus stimulating both domestic and foreign investment and, most importantly, employment.
>
> Over the medium to long-term the universal application of basic international labour standards would help to ensure a more balanced expansion of world trade and a smoother process of adjustment to changes in the global division of labour. Relatively high cost labour countries would still face the challenge of competition from low cost countries. However, that adjustment would at least be based on a broader based expansion of markets and the knowledge that the labour in competitor countries enjoyed the basic right to freedom from gross exploitation.

HANDLING THE CHANGES

Our world of work is undergoing fundamental change, both in what we work at, and the way work is organised. The changes include:

(1) A shift from agriculture to manufacturing, and then to services as the major source of employment.
(2) The knowledge content of work and of products is expanding; physical labour and raw material content is contracting; information is the new raw material.
(3) The skills' threshold of jobs is rising; the technological intensity of the economy as well as the knowledge content is also increasing.
(4) A new system of manufacturing which is very customer and quality focused, based on a highly skilled workforce using very sophisticated, flexible technology, is being created.
(5) Value added is increasingly coming from 'intangibles' or service activities, from converting knowledge into services, e.g., research, design, marketing, customer responsiveness.
(6) Innovation has become a central dynamic and a key capacity for organisations and countries.
(7) Organisations are becoming flatter, more decentralised, and more team and project based.
(8) Networks and alliances are emerging as new forms of organisation.
(9) Quality of customer service, design and uniqueness are becoming part of the definition of competitiveness.
(10) Global systems of production are now a common feature of economic activity.
(11) Learning for individuals and organisations is becoming part of the world of work.
(12) A variety of forms of work contracts are emerging.
(13) New concepts of competitiveness emerging.
(14) Constant training and upgrading of skills will be essential for survival and a central part of competitiveness in the 21st century.

While there are positive and encouraging trends in the world of work which are raising skills levels and incomes, and increasing the variety of options, there are also developments which give rise for very great concern. These include the growth in low paid employment, the casualisation and growing insecurity in many work contracts and attempts to destructure the organisation of work and segment the workforce.

CHAPTER 4

SHAPING THE FUTURE

1 – Innovation at the Heart of Work

In agricultural and industrial society, change happened slowly. Changes in knowledge, skills, jobs and products were barely noticeable. Jobs and products lasted a lifetime and change occurred over generations, with major change seen as an aberration or an expression of failure, rather than as an integral part of development. For Ireland in the 21st century, rapid and continuous change will be a characteristic and a dynamic of the world of work. It will be a built-in part of working life. The speed of change in a modern organisation and economy can be seen in the following:

* *OECD estimate that 1 in 10 jobs is lost each year in developed economies.*
* *the life of most technical knowledge is 3–4 years; organisational practices are changing continuously as new knowledge is developed*
* *the lifespan of many products is 6–18 months*
* *in affluent societies people's tastes change rapidly, forcing changes in products and in services*
* *3 out of 4 products and services which will be traded in 10 years time do not yet exist*
* *shares of employment characterised by strong knowledge base increasing rapidly.*

The 21st century economy , organised around knowledge, its creation, organisation and dissemination – will be continuously changing as knowledge changes rapidly. The globalisation of production will also change the jobs available as companies shift the elements of their production to where the comparative advantage lies. The relative comparative and competitive advantage between countries will be in continuous change as countries move to upgrade the skill levels, quality and wage levels of jobs, to move to higher levels as their economies advance. The Congress submission to the Science, Technology and Innovation Council in1994 stated:

> The speed with which governments respond to new trends, abandon obsolete policies and initiate new ones will be a primary competitive factor in the future for countries.

2 – Information – the New Raw Material

In industrial society physical labour and natural resources were the primary inputs in economic activity. In Ireland in the 21st century information will be the critical component in the functioning of the economy. As the EU points out in the White Paper on *Growth, Competitiveness, Employment* the creation, organisation and dissemination of knowledge will be the dominant feature of 21st century economies. Information technologies and advances in organisational skills have made possible the development of a system of production based on knowledge and information processing. They enable a more extensive application of knowledge throughout all aspects of the life of the economy.

Work is increasingly about the adding of value through the application of knowledge. The physical labour and traditional raw material content of the economy is decreasing. The advanced economies of the 21st century will be 'informational' in the sense that they will be structured and managed in ways which will aim to maximise knowledge-based productivity. This increased productivity will be generated through the focused application of new information and communications technologies in all parts of the economy.

3 – Science and Technology – Working for People

Science is the process of creating new knowledge on how the universe works and technology is the application of this knowledge in society. A range of new technologies are emerging to develop and apply new knowledge in society. This is resulting in an unprecedented explosion in the creation of new knowledge right across the spectrum of knowing and also in finding new ways of applying this knowledge in society.

As a result of research initiatives the knowledge base of society is doubling every 7 years. This explosion of new knowledge will be the basis of the employment of the future and of the products and services now being created. This creation is so extensive that Jacques Delors estimated that 75% of the products and services which will be traded in 10 years' time do not yet exist. This revolution in knowledge

73

creation offers very exciting possibilities and new opportunities for employment and improving people's standard of living. Because of this knowledge revolution, science, technology and innovation will play an increasingly important role in the development of society and in maintaining and generating employment.

The development of an active national policy on science and technology will need to be an important part of the preparations we make to prepare for the emerging knowledge based economy of the 21st century. This will not mean small groups of experts making decisions about buying machines or giving grants. It means the development of an awareness of the importance of science and new technology and knowledge amongst all our citizens.

Develop Awareness – Provide Resources
The process of technological development is not simply a matter of making or buying better machines. It is a cumulative, societal learning process which is closely related to the awareness and skills of people. To upgrade the innovative and technological capacity of Irish society, we need urgently to develop a much deeper awareness of the importance of science and technology throughout all aspects of our society. This should include more time and resources being devoted to science in primary and secondary schools.

More support should be given to post graduate researchers, as they form the core of the infrastructure which relates research and the economy. The availability of post graduate researchers is an important national resource which helps to attract international companies, to access international research and to generate new Irish products and services. The knowledge creating infrastructure is quickly becoming a key component in a country's capacity to attract or generate good quality employment.

At the core of the knowledge process in society is a basic infrastructure of technologies and research staff. A modern economy needs a well developed basic research infrastructure in order to generate new knowledge, to educate the research personnel needed for the invention and upgrading of products and services and to attract inward investment. Knowledge workers are a vital key to creating wealth in the future. Knowledge workers need knowledge creating facilities and organisation. Businesses which will form the core of new industries in developed economies will be primarily involved in the creation of knowledge. Development strategies should be focused on creating a supportive environment for this type of work. An interesting innovation in this knowledge infrastructure are science parks which are seen as a means of linking colleges and industry, and of generating new knowledge based industries.

There is a need to increase both private and government expenditure on research and development. It is very low by international standards, at 0.85% compared to 2–2.5% of GDP in most developed countries. The EU recommends 3% of GDP.

Dr Dave McConnell, Trinity College, Dublin, told the Centenary Conference:

> Statistics on the Irish economy give a picture that we have become, to a considerable extent, a high technology economy. But I am worried that this picture may be dangerously misleading. Much of our so-called technology is not Irish, and there is a massive void where real science should be, in our educational system.
>
> What I mean by a knowledge-based economy can be explained as follows. Most of the high technology industries in Ireland did not come here because of knowledge which was unique to Ireland. They came because of the need to have production plants inside the European Union, because of financial inducements offered by the Irish Government, and because Ireland is a stable society with a reasonably well-educated, adaptable, English-speaking labour force. These, and others were, of course, valid reasons for coming to Ireland, and they will help to keep some industry in Ireland. But we need to devise more reasons to attract international industry (and business of all kinds), to keep these industries in Ireland, and indeed to nurture indigenous high technology industry. Foremost amongst these reasons should be the quality of the scientific and technological knowledge and skills of Irish people who want to live permanently in Ireland. If we can build up such a store of highly qualified scientists and technologists, they will act as a magnet and anchor for multinational companies. In the future, industry should want to come to, and to stay in, Ireland, to take advantage of a newly created vibrant network of scientifically advanced Irish people ...

... It is my thesis that we will be much better able to attract and sustain knowledge-based industry, if we radically reform our political, social and educational attitude to science and technology. In spite of the very fine achievements of the Aer Lingus Young Scientist of the Year, and some other high points, Ireland is not yet a scientific society. An effective science system should teach science to all school students (at appropriate levels), it should teach advanced science to those school students who have an aptitude for science, it should encourage these students to study science, or applied science (medicine, agriculture, engineering, etc.) and technology at university and other third level colleges, it should stimulate the very best science students to follow scientific careers (in the same way as those with musical talent should be encouraged to become musicians), it should provide well-trained teachers and well-equipped laboratories for schools and universities, it should encourage the best university science graduates to take research degrees and support them with scholarships which are prizes worth having, and it should offer challenging research and teaching jobs to these young scientists (who could add immense brain power to our country), when they have completed their professional training. In such a society, science penetrates the culture and psyche of the society in a multitude of ways, through adult education, libraries, newspapers, radio, television, national science societies, competitions and so forth. Research scientists are expected to hold high responsibility in industries, banks, hospitals, cultural organisations, civil service, state agencies (such as the Higher Education Authority, IIRS, IDA, etc.), political parties and government ...

... We spend less on research than any country in the OECD except Turkey (which has no records), that is, we spend less than Portugal or Greece. We are frighteningly off-scale when compared to the Scandinavian countries, USA, Britain, France, Germany and the Benelux countries. The result is that our research output is also off-scale ...

... The danger is, of course, that if a country does not have a research system, it will find it very difficult to attract enough high quality scientists to work there, the few who do will quickly become disillusioned and a bad example for the young scientists, the scientific infrastructure will be impoverished in countless ways, with damaging effects on the teaching and application of science in every aspect of society, including, of course, industry. All high technology countries which are also high wage economies, have very strong scientific research systems. It is precisely these systems which are generating the ultra high technology jobs in the computer and biotechnology industries, for example, in the United States, and these industries are less likely to migrate to the low wage economies of Asia than the turnkey technologies, which are so mobile.

... We must seek out and treasure Irish brain power, be sure to educate some of it in science, stimulate it, and put it to work leading science and knowledge-based industries in a new

Ireland, where everyone will have a good basic knowledge and love of science.

The Irish Congress of Trade Unions' submission to the Advisory Council on Science, Technology and Innovation 1994 states:

> The centrality of science, innovation and knowledge in the emerging economy will mean that a policy on science, technology and innovation can no longer be just a marginal or optional aspect of government in development strategies. It needs to become a central, dynamic, informative force in government. It also needs to have a coherence and strategic focusing of funding which at present is distributed in an ad hoc manner between different areas of social and economic development.

4 – Training – An Investment that Pays Dividends

To compete in this knowledge intensive and innovative economy of the 21st century, countries are investing considerable resources in upgrading people's skills. This is not a once off activity. The pace of change and the creation of new technologies is so pervasive that investment in training will have to be ongoing as the economy will have to move constantly from old industries into new, higher productivity, high wage activities. Our view of training needs to change from seeing it as a cost, to seeing it as an investment which is an inherent part of creating the competitiveness for an economy in which people's skills and innovative commitment are the key resource.

Many commentators see the German vocational training system as a critical component of their economic success. Without a high level of skills development, Ireland will not be able to access or generate the employment of the future. Without a well developed training infrastructure, Irish companies will not be able to make the transition to new products and services which will be necessary continuously in the future.

The OECD Report on Technology and the Economy points out:

> the competitiveness of firms, areas, and nations, will, in the years ahead depend increasingly on the skills and motivation of the men and women who generate the wealth of these firms,

77

areas and nations. It is essential, therefore, that training should be looked upon not as a cost, but as an investment. It is also important that the labour force should be more systematically involved in the management, organisation and implementation of technological change, in particular through trade union intervention.

Mr Ruairi Quinn, Minister for Finance:

All our research clearly indicates that people will be the major source of innovation and competitiveness both for firms and the country as a whole. Accordingly, we will have to ensure continuous high levels of investment in education at all levels – to which people will have life long access.

In addition, we will have to develop high levels of investment in training for those already at work so that the specific skills required are available and comparable to best international practice. In a sense, learning and continuous learning becomes inherent in the jobs that people are doing.

Mr Michael Hansenne, Director General, ILO:

But the foundation of any attempt to tackle unemployment must be investment for the future: investment in education and training, in research and development, in new products, in better communications. Raising the skills of those who are already in jobs is as important as training those out of work. Competition should be based on investments in quality and innovation, with workers viewed as assets to be invested in and not just costs to be minimised.

Peter Sutherland, Director General, GATT, stated:

Governments must become more active in removing the obstacles that limit their society's capacity to adapt to change. One aspect of this is to increase investment in education, as the most basic asset people have in coping with change.

Mr Fritz Versetnitsch, President, European Trade Union Confederation, commented in his paper:

Training throughout working life must become a European right. If periods of in-company and off-premises training are to be built into working time, the exercise of that right involves setting up company training schemes negotiated with the unions to ensure that the learning process leads to real qualifications.

5 – Work: Unfreezing the Frame

Given the rate of change in products, services and knowledge, every organisation and country will need to build a strategy for innovation. This will require a proactive relationship to change as well as integrating a more dynamic image of work into its organisational culture. The innovative capacity of organisations and countries will be a key determinant of their ability to survive and prosper in the 21st century. Organisations need to produce a regular stream of new products and services. Governments need to continuously review and update development strategies. In the past, policies tended to be supported because of continuity with the past, not necessarily on the basis of relevance for the future. Organisations have tended to focus most resources on maintenance activity and less on generating new activity. Innovative capacity includes the ability to abandon old activities and policies, even while they are still successful, as well as to invent new activities.

Mr Brian Nangle, Managing Director, Munekata Ireland:

> Our challenge is how to meet the needs of change as change is presented to us. As we move into the 21st century I believe we must constantly remind ourselves that nothing is standing still; everything is relative. We can solve all problems with patience, determination and commitment. There is no fixed reference point. We must move on with new fresh thinking and a flexible approach. The twentieth century has filled our vision with an understanding of rapid change – we must use the knowledge gained wisely and with mature awareness to ensure success and harmony in the 21st century.

Companies should invest considerable resources in innovative activities to ensure the future. Frequently, jobs are lost because companies focus only on maintaining or defending existing markets and products and devote little resources to creating new markets and products. An 'innovation audit' should be an essential prerequisite for companies who receive Government assistance. Workers and their unions should be concerned that their companies are investing in the skills and research needed to produce new products. We need to develop a culture in Ireland in which management is rewarded and respected for their commitment to innovation and job retention. Shedding of staff in many cases comes from the failure to innovate and should be a source of shame, as in Japan, not of admiration, as it now is in Anglo/ USA style management prevalent in Ireland. There may be some situations where job losses are unavoidable, but a management focused on innovation will see this very much as a last, not a first, resort.

National Systems of Innovation
The process of continuously enhancing the innovative capacity of societies will now be a central task of Government. Competition between countries will be increasingly based on the quality and effectiveness of National Systems of Innovation. A National System of Innovation includes the skills and motivation of people, industrial relations systems, educational facilities, the technological infrastructure, financial institutions, fiscal and taxation policies, and the responsiveness of Government policies and institutions to change. If these elements are not open to change, operating in harmony and mutually inter-supporting then the dynamic of innovation may not happen.

In different countries different elements will be given more emphasis. For example, in Ireland because of the high dependency on multinationals for employment, the nature of the policy on multinational investment will have a critical effect on employment in Ireland. This policy is a central part of Ireland's system of innovation, and upgrading it an important part of upgrading the number and quality of jobs in Ireland.

A central part of a National System of Innovation should be Government structures actively involved in analysing industries in decline, in upgrading these industries into new products, and upgrading the workforce skills. The purpose of this initiative is to ensure a transition in companies to newer products so that employment is maintained through being recreated rather than jobs being lost and workers being unemployed. The rapid decline of old products and systems and the emergence of new products and methods of production is part of the process of modern economic development. Upgrading products and the skills of the workforce will need to be a continuous focus of Government policies in 21st century Ireland. Mechanisms which actively support transition in the economy will play a key role in development in the future. Without effective and just mechanisms, change will be resisted as people will feel the need to defend themselves against change which threatens or destroys their jobs.

A system of training and skills development for all in work must be a central part of the system of innovation. Closer ties will be needed between universities, regional colleges, FÁS, unions, businesses, and relevant government departments, to ensure a dynamic process of curriculum and skills upgrading. This will be necessary to ensure that education and training enhances the long-term employability of those in work and that businesses are involved in moving to products which are in growing markets.

The OECD points out, in its *Jobs Study:*

> long-term employment in a globalised world cannot be for OECD countries in low wages, labour intensive, standardised, products. Rather the basis for secure high wages jobs lies for them in continuously improving productivity through better education and skills and in strengthening their capacity to innovate and use new technology effectively. The primary reason for shortage of employment in OECD countries is the failure to innovate into new products and services.

The creation of innovative organisations is not achieved exclusively within organisations themselves, but also requires profound change across the culture of a society. Education and training will have a vital role to play in the cultural transformation which will be needed in order to create a truly innovative society in Ireland.

Much more extensive opportunities and a greater variety of options for education and training are needed for people in work. A particular education and training focus is needed for workers in industries in decline. This would aim to upgrade their skills to make them suitable for the transition to new products and services and prevent them becoming redundant. All the different elements of Government policies, from industrial grants to education and social welfare, should be linked in a support network. This network would act as a dynamic to create a virtuous spiral of transition in jobs which continuously raises skills levels, incomes and the quality of life. This approach would replace the vicious circle of low innovation, low skilled and defensive policies which presently permeate much of Irish management.

Ruairi Quinn, Minister for Finance, addressing the Centenary Conference, said:

> In summary, however, it is true to say that the forefront of the world's economy will increasingly concentrate upon the innovative abilities of societies and their workforces. We have already moved from a muscle to brain orientated economy which has seen many dramatic changes in patterns of work and in the very nature of the workplace itself. The next 15 years will continue to focus in upon information based and innovation driven economies. This has, I believe, enormous implications for Ireland in the future.

6 – Education to Change

The creation of innovative organisations requires a culture which is permeated by an awareness and appreciation of innovation and creativity. This awareness needs to be developed from a young age. Schools have the potential to play a crucial role in laying the foundations of a knowledge based innovative society.

a) Technology

Familiarity and 'literacy' in the use of information technology should become a central feature of the learning process in schools. Information and communications technology radically alter the learning possibilities, both in terms of materials available, methods of learning, inter-personal projects and inter-school co-operation. The technology exists to allow students work and learn with students in different countries directly through Information Highways. It is possible to access data bases and learning materials which are beyond the resources of individual schools. A deeper appreciation of the importance of science and technology should pervade the learning process. Schools will need more resources to allow them exploit the benefits of modern technology.

b) Skills and Attitudes

The 'World of Work', which most of our educational practices developed to prepare students for, is disappearing. This organisation of work valued reliability, conformity, passivity and dependency as characteristics which were most desirable in a workforce. Creativity and innovation were not part of working life for most people. Schools instilled and developed these attitudes of reliability and conformity, to fit people for individual roles in hierarchically structured organisations.

The World of Work now emerging will require a considerable degree of innovation, creativity, flexibility and ability to take personal responsibility for work. Organisations need people who can change, create and take initiatives. Part of this ability to take initiative involves the capacity to work with others as much of the new ways of working are based on project teams. The rigid and very separately defined individual whom education nurtured in the past is now becoming an organisational liability.

Learning should be structured to encourage and reward creativity and innovation in the classroom. A learning process which gives permission to make mistakes as part of learning needs to be developed. Students need to learn more about structuring their own learning as learning throughout life will be essential. Many people will have to relearn their job several times during working life or change jobs regularly. Learning and change should be seen as part of life, not as a sign of failure. The process of learning in schools should involve more team based activities so that students become familiar with the skills and stresses involved in working and negotiating with others and in forming and dissolving groups to achieve particular goals. Reflection and discussion on the learning achieved should be a significant part of each learning event.

c) Wider Knowing

The model of intelligence on which our schools curriculum has developed was based on the assumption that the rational form of knowing is superior, with consequent neglect of other aspects of intelligence. In a society where creativity and capacity to manage change are vital, other aspects of knowing need to be given attention and nurtured. The capacity of people to create, effectively manage changing interpersonal relationships and imagine and articulate desired futures, is intimately connected with an ability to use wider aspects of the personality than just rational knowing. This includes a familiarity with contacting inner feelings without the fear of losing control or being overwhelmed by these feelings. Our education trained us in a view of the world which did not validate emotions or intuition as real knowing. Listening to others, which is an essential skill for living in a learning society, is very difficult for people with little experience of their inner world, as allowing another point of view means letting go of one's boundaries and of the simplistic idea of one correct way of seeing the world.

The ability to imagine and design new products, services, and ways of working will be the most sought after skills in the future. Imaging, conceptualising, structuring, presenting projects and team working are essential learning for the future. Learning how to learn and to structure learning is as important as the specific learning content. The ability to design and upgrade a learning plan for one's life will be a core skill for people in the 21st century economy and society.

Professor Howard Gardiner, Harvard School of Education, has provided a useful classification of intelligence under 7 headings :

1. **Analytical Intelligence** – the sort we measure in IQ tests and most examinations.
2. **Pattern Intelligence** – the ability to see patterns and to create patterns – Mathematicians, Artists, often have this intelligence
3. **Musical Intelligence**

4. **Physical Intelligence** – Swimmers, Footballers, Sports people have this intelligence
5. **Practical Intelligence** – the sort of intelligence which takes a television apart and reconstructs it without knowing the parts' names
6. **Intra-Personal Intelligence** – this is also known as intuitive intelligence, an intelligence which is finely tuned to inner feelings and images as guides for knowing and planning the future
7. **Interpersonal Intelligence** – ability to get on well with others, to get things done in and through others.

All these aspects of intelligence should be validated and nurtured if we are to create the 'Intelligent Island' of the 21st century.

7 – Learning at Work

Our image and organisation of work, for the future, will include learning and upskilling as part of working life. The rigid demarcation between the world of work and the world of school or learning is obsolete. In industrial society, one left school and went to work or one did an apprenticeship and then became a fully-fledged worker. What one had learned in school or in apprenticeship lasted a lifetime with learning or retraining seen as almost a sign of failure. The workplace was where one applied knowledge previously learned.

In the knowledge based economy now emerging, learning throughout our working life will be essential for everyone, as skills and information will need to be continuously modernised. A 'time for learning' will need to become a defined part of the work contract for the future. A 'time for learning' and 'time for doing' need to become equally important parts of the world of work. Learning in work is vital for the economy as well as for individuals. The skills level of a society are decisive determinants of its ability to create and absorb new products and services. The ability to innovate is intimately inter-connected with the ability to learn. An innovative organisation or society has to be open to continuously learn new trends in demand and new ways of doing and

85

creating. It also has to be able to forget. This forgetting involves individuals abandoning old skills and attitudes and organisations giving up obsolete products and strategies. Learning will have to be a central part of the culture. Many commentators see the learning organisations as the organisation of the future. Learning organisations will need individuals who are committed to and skilled in learning.

In the rapidly changing world the ability to learn and to structure learning will be critical, not alone for individuals or businesses but for all organisations and countries. The capacity of a country to learn and respond will be very important in the 21st century. Paradoxically, Ireland's small size may be a competitive advantage as it enables an intimacy of inter-relationships which can facilitate quick collective action or response. The old historical image of Ireland as a centre of learning may also help to develop an awareness of Ireland as a learning and intelligent island in a world where intelligence is the key force.

8 – Learning Organisations

The creating of organisations which are effective at learning, innovating and making use of new emerging opportunities involves new skills and commitments. These skills can vary from identifying opportunities for using information technologies to enhancing organisational learning. They also include more human skills of listening and learning from others, giving and receiving information and new, more co-operative and less competitive patterns of relationship. Loosening of the boundaries of organisations to facilitate the easier flow of ideas and people will also be important. Abandoning obsolete skills, products and strategies is an important part of the learning process.

Mr Brian L. Nangle, Irish Industrialist and Director, Munekata Ireland Ltd, described this learning process:

> Awareness is a function of how much we are prepared to pick up knowledge or information, how open we are to being influenced and how well we listen. Do we hear and understand, or do we reject what we intuitively or emotionally want not to accept? Good decisions are based on knowledge; great decisions are based, I believe, on awareness and sensitivity.

The learning and innovation capacity of organisations is not driven by edicts but by the strength of the learning desires of the members. The motivation of individuals to maintain and upgrade their skills and to enhance their employability can be a powerful incentive to upgrade the culture of organisations.

For the workforce, the failure of the organisation to provide training threatens their present job and also their long-term employability. If one is not learning new skills, then one is falling back, losing in employability and earning power as the skills threshold of work is rising and new technologies and organisational practices are emerging at an accelerating rate.

9 – Competitiveness – A New Definition

The definition of competitiveness for companies and countries needs to evolve as the national and global economy evolves. There is a great deal of talk about the need for business to become more competitive. In Ireland, increasing competitiveness is generally presented as being synonymous with levels of wages – becoming competitive means lowering wages or reducing staff numbers.

The identification of competitiveness with levels of wages also tends to see products as competing primarily on costs, with lower prices giving products competitive advantage. This identification of competitiveness with levels of wages and price is based on a concept of an economy which is out of touch with the modern world of OECD economies and relates more to developing countries' economies. Industries where price and wage levels are the primary determinants of competitiveness are industries of the mass production era, competing on costs with other standardised products and using production systems based on intensive inputs of unskilled labour and low technology.

In modern OECD economies the goods and services in growth areas are aimed at niche markets where other factors like quality, uniqueness and customer responsiveness are as important, or more important, than price. With some of these products, higher prices are signs of status. Standardised products, where the price is the defining competitive factor, are either produced by highly automated systems or in developing countries. For modern companies the skills and motivation of the workforce are a central definition of their competitiveness. The workforce is the central asset of a company, not a cost. The intellectual capacity and innovative commitment of a workforce are now key determinants of companies' competitiveness.

For countries, the classical idea of competitiveness has been a very passive one based on the inherited unchanging supply of labour and raw materials. Countries specialised in products which were related to their inherited comparative advantage.

In the concept of competitiveness now emerging, countries create, not inherit, the factors which give them competitive advantage. It is a much more dynamic and broader concept of competitiveness. Countries which will prosper in the 21st century will be actively upgrading and redefining the factors which can give them competitive advantage with new factors being continuously identified. The skills and motivation of the workforce are seen as central to modern competitiveness. The banking system is also seen as critical.

A major factor attributed to the success of Japanese and German economies is the relationship between banks and business. The policy on finance for business in both these countries is very different than in the Anglo/USA model, within which we function in Ireland. In Japanese and German systems, banks take a much longer and wider view of the returns on investment in companies. Upgrading the capacity of Irish businesses' competitiveness must involve developing a longer term culture in relation to investment policy in business.

The training systems are now critical elements of countries' competitiveness, as countries are moving to upgrade workforce skills and capacities to absorb and develop new technologies. The quality of industrial relations locally and nationally is equally important. The capacity to innovate is recognised as the key capacity determining the competitiveness of countries, and industrial relations play a key role in determining that capacity. Changes in the exchange values of currencies are becoming increasingly important determinants of the competitiveness of countries. Employment in Europe points out that it is 'exchange rate movements rather than differentials in productivity or wage rates which have been the major determinant of the cost competitiveness of European producers relative to those in the rest of the world as well as between producers in different European countries. Social cohesion is seen as an important part of competitiveness in many European countries.

Upgrading our understanding of competitiveness of companies and countries will be an important part of the process of creating an employment strategy for 21st century Ireland.

CHAPTER 5

THE NEW WORLD OF WORK

1 – A Different Image

The image of organisations which pervaded industrial society was that of a machine composed of separate and defined parts controlled from a centre which identified problems and fixed them. The world in which it functioned was a static one. This image is not suitable for the type of organisations we will need in the Ireland of the 21st century.

Organisations need to be imagined as living systems, where co-ordination is horizontal rather than vertical between different autonomous units. Organisations learn about their environment through information exchanges across permeable boundaries in a continuous process.

Self-organising networks and decentralised value adding webs are replacing hierarchical, stand alone, machines as the image of modern organisations.

2 – More Variety

The single model of organisation as the traditional, hierarchical structure providing the same goods or service in the same way over long periods of time is becoming absorbed within a wide variety of organisational forms. It is now just one model of a way of working suited to particular markets and products.

In the next century, it is unlikely that any one new model will emerge, as organisations are being designed and redesigned to serve a society which is rapidly evolving and is much more diverse and varied than in the past in its tastes and technologies. Promoting and supporting diversity is one of the hallmarks of the emerging economy and society.

Despite the likelihood of considerable organisational variety, a number of characteristics which organisations will share can be identified.

3 – Flatter Structures

A number of trends are reducing the layers of decision-making in organisations resulting in flatter organisational structures.

(a) The emergence of the computer and the evolution of

information technologies has greatly expanded the possibilities for organisational architecture. In the hierarchical model of organisation many people were employed in relaying information within the organisation. This was generally from the top to the bottom. Edicts come from the bosses, who had the ideas, to the workers below who carried them out. Reports were sent upwards on how those below were working. Information technology does away with the need for layers of supervisors and middle managers or human information carriers.

(b) In the emerging knowledge based, innovative economy workers bring their intelligence as well as their bodies to work. The intelligence and the creative commitment of the workforce is becoming the key resource of organisations. Flatter, more participatory structures are seen to be more effective means of developing people's commitment and creativity. Because of the rapidity of changes in the types of goods and services in demand and in the ways of producing and delivering them, organisations need to be able to respond more rapidly and change what they do and the way they do it more flexibly than in the past. The long chain of command of hierarchical structures is not generally as flexible as flatter organisations.

4 – More Decentralisation

Information and communications technologies reduce distance to zero. People can be instantaneously inter-connected over any distance. This allows for people to be located long distances from each other and still work together on projects. Concepts like virtual organisation and virtual communities are now being used to describe networks of people who inter-act through computers or multimedia systems but rarely, or never, meet. People now consider themselves as communities through these connections; Internet is the best known of the networks.

In a more practical sense, organisations are using the advances in technologies and organisational practices to build large organisations from a series of decentralised units. Once these units reach 100/200 people, the parent organisation creates a new self contained subsidiary as a more effective means of managing. A small core of central staff co-ordinate these decentralised units. This is seen as a means of organisations becoming more flexible, e.g., ABB Asea Brown Boveri – a £30 billion electrical engineering company is composed of 1,300 separate operating companies.

The goal is to be simultaneously local and global, big and small, centralised and decentralised. These types of organisations are horizontally and hierarchically interconnected. They focus on giving initiative to the local rather than the centre, to empower the local. Decisions are taken nearest to the place they affect, with subsidiarity of decision-making as the goal. Responsibility grows upwards from teams. Active inter-personal, inter-company, inter-project sharing of information is the essential glue which binds the organisation. Many large organisations are becoming webs of small companies or profit centres.

5 – Networking and Alliances
Large companies are redesigning their structures into more web-like structures as a means of combining the advantages of the flexibility of smallness with the economies of scale of largeness. Project teams can be composed of workers from different locations in a country or around the globe, e.g., Digital engineers all over the world are linked in a company network. Kodak connect design, engineering and manufacturing personnel within local area networks to create product teams. Internet connects 50 million people in an electronic network.

In addition to information networks created globally, there are numerous initiatives under way creating local development networks, integrating businesses, libraries, schools, hospitals and local government

A significant innovation in economic development is the growing attention to inter-firm and inter-organisation alliances as ways of doing business. Increasingly, companies form alliances to undertake joint projects. Often companies will form co-operative alliances with companies whom they compete with in other areas. In addition to individual companies forming alliances, groups of companies form alliances, e.g., in the automobile industry, General Motors has a network of partners which include Toyota, Isuzu, Mizuki and Saab. This network competes globally with the Ford network of Ford, Nissan and Jaguar. Similar types of networks are formed in other industries, including computers, aerospace and the communications industries.

Inter-firm alliances are a very common part of development strategies. Small companies share information or resources to achieve economies of scale. Alliances between small and large firms are also common as large firms access small firms' innovations, and use their finance and marketing power to create markets. There are many examples of towns, cities, regions, forming trans-European alliances as a means of the local community having more active involvement in their own development.

The result of this growth of alliances as ways of doing business is that people and organisations need to more actively co-operate with others than they did previously. The concept of the stand alone cowboy style 'entrepreneur' or organisation competing against the rest of the world is becoming an obsolete mode of development. In addition to more inter-organisational co-operation, the reality of organisations co-operating in one area and competing in another is common. The result is that individuals and organisations have to learn new skills and attitudes which encourage a different balance between co-operation and competition than in the past.

While we in Ireland talk quite a lot about co-operation, in practice we are not very good co-operators, as we are educated to be individualised, separate and competitive. Organisations similarly have been structured with tight boundaries, to give very clear and separate definitions. Within organisations individual's roles were also clear, defined and separate with each carrying out an aspect of a defined task. Inter-personal, co-operative and inter-active communications were not part of the culture of organisations. For the future within organisations and between organisations, inter-personal sharing will be part of the work culture. Indeed, in a knowledge based organisation, the intensity and frequency of inter-personal sharing will be an integral dynamic of the process of creating and doing business. Inter-organisational alliances will be part of the structure of work.

This changing balance between co-operation and competition and the growth in networking means that a significant part of an organisation's competitive skills and capacity will be their abilities in project working, inter-firm co-operation and collaboration. This inter-personal and inter-firm co-operation will require that people and organisations learn how to function with much looser boundaries than in the past and become more skilled in cross boundary negotiations.

6 – Industrial Districts

A particularly interesting and important networking innovation in business and regional development is the concept of industrial districts which emerged in northern Italy and has been replicated in many places. This development is seen as a central reason for the success of northern Italy in the past 25 years. The strength of this process depends on the quality and the persistence of the inter-action that happens between small firms in a district. There is an active sharing of information and creation of temporary alliances of firms providing specific inputs into the creation of new products.

Industrial districts are not a passive collection of firms on industrial estates but are characterised by a particular awareness of the benefits of strong networks and inter-firm co-operation. A small firm in an industrial district does not stand alone – a condition of its success is the success of the whole network of firms of which it is a part. The success of development policies in industrial districts is evaluated in terms of the growth of the community of firms rather than individual firms.

At present Irish business culture is permeated by a communication system where others are seen as competitors for a fixed amount of goods in a static economy of unchanging products. The creation of more active inter-personal and inter-firm co-operation involves the creation of a different system of communication. This means creating an awareness among people and organisations that in an innovation-driven society it is important that ideas and information are shared. In an innovative society the expansion of wealth depends on people supporting each others' efforts to be creative.

7 – New Systems of Communication

The system of communication in the mass production hierarchical organisation was designed to enforce conformity, control and standardised behaviour. People operated a dominant/dependency type of communications, where they were either dominant or dominated.

The communication systems now developing are based on the assumption that the intelligence of each person is a resource for the other. It is a win/win view of organisational communication. The quality of the products of an organisation are an expression of the level of the intelligence of that organisation. This intelligence is created through the commitment and quality of the inter-actions of the members. Each tries to communicate, not as a means of control, but of adding value to the skills or the contribution of the other person, thereby opening the door to new possibilities for their energies and intelligence.

8 – Teams and Projects

The trend towards basing work on teams and projects will have a significant impact on most people's experience of work in the next century. This development has been influenced by the success of the Japanese (particularly in the automobile industry) in raising productivity, innovation, responsiveness and quality through organisational structures based on teams. An important part of this success has been the ability of Japanese management to get the involvement and commitment of their workforce. The overall aim is to get workers to take more responsibility for their work. Many commentators feel that the achievement of this type of environment has been possible because of the level of trust and security which the culture of Japanese business and the life-long employment contract provides.

A similar focus on trust pervades German business culture. In contrast, in Irish business culture companies see their primary, if not their exclusive responsibility, as the maximisation of profits for investors and are judged solely on their ability to do this. The Japanese view of a company is more one of a community of people, rather than simply a mechanism for shareholders' profit. The stakeholders include the employees, management, shareholders, suppliers, and banks. Profitability is looked at from a much broader perspective than in the Anglo/American model within which we operate. Employees are considered to be the most important stakeholders, and people are hired for careers, not jobs.

One example of this wider commitment was the way the restructuring of Nippon Steel in 1984 was undertaken to ensure that the community of people in Nippon Steel had a good future. The response to loss-making was a plan which aimed to increase company growth by increasing sales in non-steel business to 50% of sales, moving into engineering, new materials, biotechnology and even tourism. This was based on an extensive programme of learning by employees of new expertise.

For most Irish companies the response to loss due to market change is to cut back staff until the company is back in profit. Short term profitability is often the sole guiding criterion. This approach causes a lack of trust in the workforce. The results of down-sizing is that the company, while it appears to have made progress by getting back to profit, loses the key resources for successful development in the long-term – its staff.

Many organisations are now structuring work by combining staff in teams to undertake projects. Management need to develop the new skill of putting people together in suitable combinations and providing them with the environmental support and space to undertake the projects. These organisations are a portfolio of people's competencies and intelligence, combining in temporary and changing combinations, inventing, creating and delivering goods and services through focused teams. Some managers see team working as simply a means of getting workers to do more for less and thereby negate the long-term potential of team work.

9 – New Packaging

The packaging of working time is becoming less standardised. The traditional 'standard' work contract of the 40 hour, 40 year package is being complemented by a growth in part time work, short term contract work, self employment and temporary work. Organisations are tending to have a variety of staff contracts with a mixture of full-time, part-time, permanent, temporary and project contracts.

The impetus for this variety is coming from a number of motivations – the speed of change of technologies, consumer tastes and the variety of goods and services on offer are resulting in organisations wanting more flexibility in terms both of staff numbers and skills. This flexibility can be motivated and organised to enhance work and enable the employment of more people in better jobs. It can also be motivated and organised as a means of reducing the negotiating power of workers, breaking their sense of solidarity and leaving them open to exploitation.

The changing balance of the numbers of men and women in the workforce is also a factor in the new packaging of work. Changes in people's values in relation to work are also affecting work structures. New technologies have greatly expanded the possibilities of variety in the packaging of work.

10 – Part-time Work

Non-standardised forms of work contracts are more common in the growing sectors of the economy than in the declining sectors. The extent of part-time work varies within Europe. In Ireland the percentage of people in part-time work is lower than in Europe generally although it has grown from 5% of the workforce in 1980 to 8% in 1991. The Netherlands with 31% has the highest percentage of people in part-time jobs – almost all new work is part-time as it is used as a way of sharing jobs. The German Government is also promoting part-time working as a way of sharing work. Women account for the vast bulk of part-time workers – 85% of all part-time work in the EU is done by women.

In recognition of the importance of non-standard work contracts the EU recently introduced a directive to give part-time workers the same rights and protection as full-time workers. It is very disappointing to hear Irish employers opposing these developments which are aimed at promoting social justice in Europe. It is a sad reflection of Irish employers' lack of belief in their ability to create and compete with other Europeans, while paying decent wages and maintaining high social standards. It would appear that they see themselves as only able to operate in industries which compete on the basis of low wages and low social standards. It is important that trade unions work to encourage a higher belief in employers in their creative ability to compete in the higher value adding industries with higher social standards.

11 – Gathered Organisations

Some vociferous commentators predict that the capacity for global inter-connectiveness is going to bring a complete destructuring of organisations. This, they claim, will result in almost everyone working alone in their homes and telecommuting via information highways. This is presented as a liberating vision by some. However, for many people it is a very worrying scenario, as it presents the likelihood of a loss of much of the social fabric of work and the opportunities for inter-personal inter-action which are so important for a healthy society.

For most people an important aspect of work is the experience of participating with others in the process of defining and achieving goals. The inter-actions which take place during this participation are an important part of the development of people's personalities. This need is so fundamental to human beings that considerable attention should be given to ensuring that employment opportunities are created in gathered organisations. The culture of civil society is an important part of the competitiveness of European society.

In a knowledge society it is through conversations and sharing ideas that new employment and wealth creating ideas emerge. People need direct personal inter-action for this. Research shows a resistance to teleworking in Europe compared to the US. While the advocates of individual working see this as a fault needing to be rectified, it can also be seen as an awareness by Europeans of the importance for them of the social dimension of work which they see as an important part of their culture.

12 – Knowledge – Content Expanding

The goods and services which are beginning to dominate the emerging economy are more knowledge intensive and less labour and raw material intensive than those which dominated industrial society. As Peter Drucker points out the pattern of the decrease in raw materials can be seen in the fact that, while the output of Japanese manufacturing has doubled in the past 25 years, the use of raw materials and energy has not increased.

In physical terms, it can also be seen in the difference between the material content of the central feature of the industrial revolution – the steam engine, and the central feature of industry now – the microchip. The decline in the direct labour content and costs in manufacturing can be seen in the decline in blue collar work. Again according to Peter Druker, further evidence can be found in the decline in direct labour costs in manufacturing, from 60–70% in the 1950s down to 10% of total costs in 1990.

Many of the new products and services now being traded have little or no material content and are composed of pure information, knowledge or relationships. Examples of these products include medicines, financial services, films and computer chips. The main sources of value added and costs in modern products are in intangibles like research and development, imaging, design, packaging, legal, accounting, marketing and quality of relationships.

For example, in medicine, the direct labour costs and rewards to routine labour or raw material costs of producing pills is relatively small. The physical content of a pill is also minute – it is the stored intelligence which is giving the major value. The costs of producing it can be £100s of millions. However, the higher proportion of costs are in research and development, patents, marketing, etc., not in the manufacturing or the raw materials. Similarly, with films, financial services, health services, computer software, social services, education and leisure, there is little or no material content.

This increased knowledge content is occurring across the whole range of products which form the core of goods and services traded in developed economies. Competitiveness is being redefined around the knowledge content, rather than the labour or raw material content of products. Business focuses on increasing the information content of products as a way of adding value, e.g., plans are developing in many countries to create intelligent motorways which will provide a range of information to motorists using new information technologies. Already, we can see the start of this process with information displayed for motorists on routes into Dublin about the number of empty spaces available in different city centre car parks.

The growing importance of the knowledge content and of knowledge workers is being reflected in the costs structure of products with a decline in the share going to routine labour and an increasing share going to the knowledge adding workers. For example, 85% of the price of a microchip goes to designers, copyrights and engineering, with only 6% to routine labour. The biggest beneficiaries of the knowledge expansion of the economy are those whose business is the creation of knowledge. The depth of knowledge intensity of many new products is such that commentators now see business as best understood from the perspective of being primarily the creation, organisation and dissemination of knowledge rather than the physical production of goods.

13 – New Sources of Employment

Education
Health
Personal Services
Tourism
Service to Business – e.g., Design, Marketing, Research,
                    Intangibles
Culture – e.g., Arts, Theatre, Festivals, Music
Environment – e.g., Urban Renewal
Audio-Visual, Films
Computer Software
Computer Hardware
Sport
Music
Bio-Technology – e.g., Genetic Engineering
Aerospace
Financial Services
Caring Services – e.g., For people who are older

Many of these new 'industries' have no material content and are based on information, images and relationships. Even farmers are increasingly becoming knowledge workers. Knowledge workers add value to information. Information workers process information.

14 – Skills Levels Rising

There is a shift towards a higher skill and informational content in new jobs in Ireland and other OECD countries There is a decline in blue collar, unskilled and semi-skilled jobs and a growth in white collar jobs. There is a general thrust towards a white collar labour force moving towards the higher tier in terms of skills and income. There is an across the board rise in the threshold of competence required for employment. This is primarily due to the higher knowledge and skills content of much new work. Managerial, professional and technical categories of work are growing fastest. Service jobs in lower income and skill categories like sales, clerical, and waitering are also growing, but growth is much slower

**Employment shares for blue- and white-collar workers,
1981 and 1991**

% of total employment

	BLUE COLLAR		WHITE COLLAR	
	1981	1991	1981	1991
Australia	36.3	35.6	56.6	59.4
Austria	36.4	34.8	54.1	57.1
Belgium	35.3	32.9	61.1	63.4
Canada	29.5	24.5	65.1	71.1
Denmark	31.6	29.8	65.4	65.1
Finland	29.5	25.2	58.5	64.7
Germany	35.4	31.9	58.4	61.5
Greece	30.8	29.5	39.5	47.5
Ireland	**28.9**	**27.6**	**53.6**	**58.0**
Japan	37.8	35.0	52.1	57.9
Netherlands	24.6	24.2	68.1	70.5
New Zealand	29.0	24.9	59.9	65.3
Norway	31.9	26.1	58.5	65.9
Portugal	37.3	32.6	33.8	47.6
Spain	39.0	37.1	42.8	51.7
Sweden	31.2	28.3	63.2	68.2
Turkey	–	25.3	–	28.2
United Kingdom	30.7	28.4	65.3	68.6
United States	28.2	26.0	68.1	71.1
Unweighted average	32.4	29.5	53.9	60.1

Source: Employment Outlook, OECD, 1994, p. 82.

than in the higher income and skilled occupational categories.

An OECD report on a recent study ranking jobs in the
USA according to skills found only 27% of all new jobs fell
into the two lowest skill categories, while 40% of current jobs
require these skills. By contrast, 41% of new jobs were in the
three highest skill groups, compared to only 24% of current
jobs. The high skill jobs include scientists, lawyers, engineers, managers, accountants, teachers. Low skill category
jobs include transport workers, machine workers, hand-
workers, helpers and labourers. A Canadian study has
shown that business sector employment was stronger in
high technology, high knowledge content industries than in
other industries. The employment growth in high knowledge industries was 2.5 times that of medium knowledge
industries and 4 times that of low knowledge industries.

Employment changes by occupational groups in Ireland, 1981–1990

Occupation	Absolute Change	% Change
Professionals	28,200	+36.8
Associate Professionals	8,300	+17.7
Personal Service Workers	9,100	+14.7
Managers/Proprietors	13,100	+13.9
Sales Workers	5,600	+7.6
Security Workers	–100	–0.2
Foremen	–5,400	–3.2
Skilled Maintenance	–2,300	–4.0
Clerical Workers	–6,700	–4.3
Transport Workers	–3,200	–6.3
Other Skilled Workers	–6,700	–7.2
Semi-skilled & Operatives	–10,000	–10.1
Agricultural Workers	–22,600	–11.8
Labourers & Others	–19,200	–32.1
Total	–11,900	–1.1

Source: 'Employment Trends and Labour Market Issues in the 1990's', by Donal A. Dineen in Labour Market Review, FÁS, 1994, p. 7.

The rise in the skills levels of occupations is also being caused by the higher educational levels of the population. In many areas the resultant competition for jobs is pushing up the educational levels of jobs beyond the levels needed to do the jobs. This may cause considerable problems in the future, if jobs do not provide the level of challenge or opportunities needed by this increasingly higher educated workforce. In all OECD countries, there is a declining demand for lower skilled people. This is becoming a major social problem.

The sectors of employment in which the rate of job creation has been strongest throughout Europe are the sectors where the average level of educational attainment is highest. The sectors where employment declined most were where educational requirements are lowest, like agriculture and unskilled manufacturing. There will be an increasing need for a more highly educated workforce to fill the jobs being created. In the areas to have generated significant new jobs in the EU – banking, insurance, business services, health and education – a high percentage of those employed had post-compulsory educational qualifications.

Educational attainment of the workforce (25+) by sector in the Community, 1991

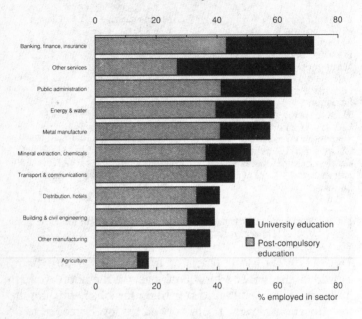

Source: *Employment in Europe, Commission of the European Communities, 1991, p. 104.*

15 – Services the Main Growth Area

As economies develop, the major source of employment shifts from agriculture to manufacturing and then to services. Services are predicted to be the main source of new employment in Ireland and Europe in the 21st century.

In OECD countries between 1920 and 1970, there was a huge decline in agricultural employment with economies becoming 'post agricultural'. From 1970–1990 there was a similarly large decline in manufacturing employment and expansion in services as economies became 'post industrial'. In Ireland in 1980–1991 agricultural employment fell by 30% and industrial employment by 15%. Most of the jobs growth during the 1980s occurred in services such as finances and business services (8%) and community and personal services

Sectoral employment trends in the Community 1965–1989

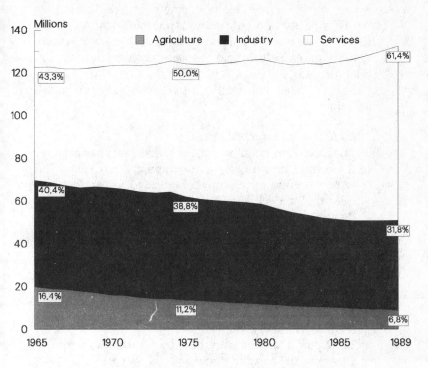

Source: *Employment in Europe, Commission of the European Communities, 1991, p. 31.*

(30%). For example, there are now more people employed in business services than in farming.

In the EU, over 2 million people are employed in leisure, arts and culture – as many as in the whole motor car industry and more than in the production of clothing and footwear. In Ireland the arts sector of the economy has a gross revenue of around £450 million providing the equivalent of up to 21,500 full-time jobs and a minimum export value of £100 million. Fifty per cent more are employed in personal services, such as hairdressing or dry cleaning than in iron and steel production. Services now account for 2 out of 3 jobs in OECD countries.

The decline in agriculture and industry as the major sources of employment has not come from a decline in productive capacity or a failure in output in agriculture or industry. It has come from a combination of the increased productivity of agriculture and industry, changes in organisational methods and growth in demand for new kinds of services, e.g., video libraries, computer maintenance, adult education.

(a) Increased Productivity

The long-term trend over the past 150 years has been for the output of agriculture and industry to expand but with a decline in the numbers needed to produce this output. The decline in numbers employed is primarily due to increased productive capacity as new knowledge, new skills and new technology have been applied more intensively to the process of production. Technology is stored knowledge. The workforce in agriculture and industry is becoming involved in the application of knowledge, rather than of physical labour.

(b) Changes in Organisation

Changes in the organisation of production are also changing the relative importance of services as sources of employment. There has been a statistical recategorising of many activities which were formerly categorised as manufacturing into the services category. Many companies either subcontract these activities to other companies or locate them in different parts of the globe within the same company. The activities include both high wage jobs like design, accounting, legal affairs, research, marketing and lower wage jobs like security, cleaning, catering, data processing.

(c) Demand for new Services

Another reason for the expansion of services as a source of employment is the demand for new services arising from increased affluence, new technologies, higher

Long-term trends in employment share by sector
as a % of total employment

	Agriculture	Industry	Services		Agriculture	Industry	Services
France				**Germany**			
1901	41.4	31.5	27.1	1907	33.9	39.9	26.2
1949	29.6	33.1	37.3	1950	22.1	44.7	33.2
1960	22.0	36.9	41.1	1960	13.8	47.7	38.5
1970	13.3	38.7	47.9	1970	8.5	48.4	43.1
1980	8.6	35.4	56.0	1980	5.2	42.8	52.0
1990	6.1	29.2	64.6	1990	3.5	39.1	57.4
Italy				**Japan**			
1901	61.7	22.3	16.0	1906	61.8	16.2	22.0
1951	43.9	29.5	26.7	1950	48.3	22.6	29.0
1960	32.2	36.2	31.6	1960	32.6	29.7	37.6
1970	19.6	38.4	42.0	1970	17.4	35.7	46.9
1980	13.9	36.9	49.2	1980	10.4	35.3	54.2
1990	8.7	31.6	59.7	1990	7.2	34.1	58.7
United Kingdom				**United States**			
1901	13.0	43.9	43.1	1900	40.4	28.2	31.4
1951	5.0	47.4	47.6	1950	12.8	31.5	55.7
1961	3.7	48.4	47.9	1960	8.6	30.6	60.8
1970	3.2	44.1	52.7	1970	4.4	33.0	62.6
1980	2.6	37.2	60.3	1980	3.5	29.9	66.6
1990	2.1	28.7	69.2	1990	2.8	25.7	71.5

Source: The OECD Jobs Study, Evidence and Explanation, Part II, The Adjustment Potential of the Labour Market, OECD, 1994, p. 5.

levels of education and the ageing of the population. The growth in affluence means that societies can attend to a wider variety and more sophisticated range of needs than in the past. New technologies and knowledge enable the creation of new services and products which are less material in content, e.g., films and videotapes. The ageing of the population is also leading to the need for new services, e.g., travel, health and leisure.

An interesting breakdown of services was compiled by M. Cassells and Y. Aoyama in an analysis of the employment structure of the seven leading industrial countries 1970–1990, published by the ILO in *Labour Market Review*.

The breakdown of service employment they classified as:

% of Total Employment

Producer Services	7–14%
Social Services	20–25%
Distributive Services including Retail	20–25%
Personal Services	10–14%

Producer Services – these are services to business which are considered critical in a modern economy and include accountants, lawyers, designers, economists and engineers.

Social Services – include activities like health, education, care for aged and culture.

Distributive Services – include transport, communication, wholesale and retail services.

Personal Services – include restaurants, bars and leisure.

Robert Reich, United States Minister for Labour, does away with distinctions of work between agriculture, manufacturing and services, and defines work under three new categories:

1. Routine Production Services – Declining in number
Task: Repetitive task in high volume manufacturing; also routine supervisory or managerial jobs.

Skills: Reliability, capacity to take directions
Pay: Pay is function of hours worked or amount of work done
Future: One quarter of jobs declining due to automation, reorganisation or Third World competition. Low pay as in competition with low wage countries' cost structures for standardised products.

2. In Person Services – Growing in number

Task: Provided person to person – sales, hotels, social services, health, education.
Skills: Reliability, good inter-personal skills.
Pay: Both high and low wage activities; pressure on pay of low skilled due to competition for jobs from displaced routine workers.
Future: Growing

3. Symbolic Analytic Services – Growing in Number

Task: Problem solving, identifying, strategic brokering
Pay: Value placed on new designs and concepts grows relative to value placed on standard products.
Income not on quantity or time but on quality, originality and cleverness with which they solve problems or identify new problems.
Traded world wide; not in competition with low wage standardised activities.
Future: 20% of jobs – numbers growing rapidly.

In the high value added enterprise the claims of both routine labour and financial capital are subordinated increasingly to the claims of those who solve, identify and broker new problems.

According to Robert Reich a diminishing share of every pound spent in advanced economies has gone to production workers over the past decade. Those who conceptualise the problems have commanded higher salaries. This suggests development strategies for countries in the future should be based on maximising the numbers of symbolic analysts as these are the people who are creating the new high value products and services, and command high salaries. These activities are not easily duplicated in less developed economies, and are traded internationally thereby generating wealth for a country.

Services

The images we tend to have of work are that good jobs are in manufacturing, and services provide low paid, insecure employment in fast food restaurants, cleaning, shops and security. While there has been a growth in these lower paid jobs, they still comprise a relatively small percentage of overall jobs (10–15%) in a modern economy. Skill intensive, high paying service jobs have grown faster, and wages in services have grown faster than in manufacturing. Professor Kenneth Galbraith sees the organisation of service workers as the next big challenge for trade unions, as the organisation of service work is often very different than that in traditional sources of trade union membership. He told the Conference:

> In the modern world much of the old mass-production industry has yielded to technology, or it has gone to the new industrial lands, where at low wage cost, it employs workers recently recruited from the worse privations of primitive peasant agriculture. Left in the advanced countries are the geographically immobile service industries; these scatter workers in minute number over the whole social terrain. They are no longer brought together for communal action, as in the case of traditional industry.
>
> There is also the movement into the higher levels of technology. Also into design and the arts, to entertainment and to a large range of cultural and intellectual activities. Many so employed have a far higher level of individual aspiration than the original industrial worker. This is not so urgently served by the traditional union. All of these developments are unfavourable to organisation in its original, its classical, form.

16 – Manufacturing Still Important

While services have grown in every developed economy, this does not mean the demise of manufacturing as an important source of employment. It still provides 30% of employment in most developed economies and 25% of GNP. The relative levels of employment in manufacturing and services is quite varied within the OECD. Both Japan and Germany have maintained high levels of employment in manufacturing, with Japan still expanding. During the period 1970–1990 manufacturing employment in Japan increased by 4% and in the USA by 1.5% while in the EU there was a decline of 20%.

The reason for this trend is that Japan has moved to manufacturing high technology products which are growing strongly, while European industry is still overly dependent on low technology products. Within manufacturing, there have been different employment patterns emerging for different industries. In OECD countries, employment in high range, high technology manufacturing has expanded since 1970 while in medium technology it has remained stable. Employment has dropped heavily in low wage, low technology sectors.

Most OECD countries are moving from low tech to high tech sectors. Most European countries are still located in lower tech products compared with the USA and Japan. Total manufacturing dropped within the EU because of the concentration of European business in relatively lower technology sectors, which are in decline. This is especially true of Irish indigenous industry, which is heavily concentrated in these low tech sectors which are in decline as sources of employment. As the OECD *Jobs Study* points out, a major cause of unemployment is the failure of business to innovate, to create new products and new sources of employment.

Most of the trade of OECD countries occurs within the OECD area, which specialises in high technology, high wage industries. The composition of OECD exports has shifted in the last two decades towards high and medium technology industries and high and medium wage industries, and away from labour intensive and resource intensive sectors.

Expanding Industries
Since 1970 employment in manufacturing expanded in high wage/high growth and high technology industries. These include:

Computers, office equipment, aerospace, motor vehicles,

pharmaceuticals, electronics (communications) equipment, semi-conductors, instruments, rubber, plastic, chemicals, paper products, printing and publishing.

Declining Industries

Declining manufacturing employment is mainly in low wage, labour intensive industries which include:

Textiles, footwear and leather, tobacco, wood, cork, furniture, fabricated metals, iron and steel.

Employment change by Sector (%), Ireland 1991–1997

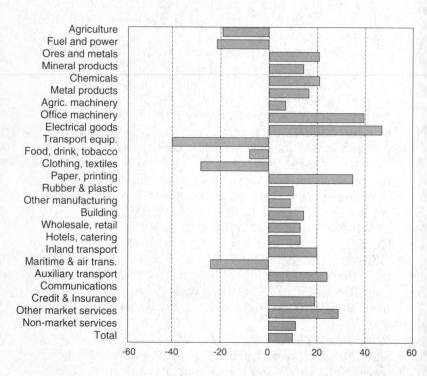

Source: 'Labour Market Outlook and the Structure of Employment in Ireland in 1997' by John Fitzgerald and Gerard Hughes in Labour Market Review, FÁS, 1994, p. 38.

17 – New System of Manufacturing

A new system of manufacturing is being created which is likely to dominate in the 21st century. This is resulting from the combination of changes in information technology and new organisational practices. It is a system of production which is based on highly flexible technologies integrated with highly skilled workers and organised in small teams. This system of production is called a variety of names – Lean, TQM, Quick Response Manufacturing, etc. Its design draws heavily on the Japanese experience. It has a flat organisation structure in contrast to the hierarchical, authoritarian Taylorist form of organisation for mass production. More responsibility and authority is given to the workforce as a means of improving the organisation's responsiveness to changes in demands. A central focus in the design of this system is to be able to respond quickly to rapidly changing customer demand. It aims to produce a wider variety of products in shorter runs and compete for more niche and quality markets than mass production where cost is the dominant competitive factor and products are standardised.

Workers in the new system require a broader range of skills than in mass production systems. These include technical skills to work with complex technologies, computer skills, cognitive and social skills, including abstract and conceptual thinking and understanding group dynamics and inter-personal skills. Much of the work in this system involves redesigning and improving the process. Therefore it involves a lot of initiative and responsibility throughout the workforce. It makes extensive use of 'intelligent' technologies and focuses a lot of resources in design, quality and responsiveness.

The development of this system in manufacturing creates new, highly skilled jobs with engineering and technical skills and reduces demand for semi-skilled and unskilled labour. It also creates demands for new jobs in 'intangibles' or service jobs of design, research, packaging, marketing and consumer research. It is in these areas of service that most of value added now takes place. Organisational capacity is now a prime determinant of competitiveness.

This system is resulting in the redesign of many traditional industries into higher quality, more niche, higher costs markets, e.g., watches, clothes, shoes. It is only through this upgrading of products, skills and technologies that these industries can survive in the longer term, as the GATT agreement allows much freer access of products, particularly textiles and leather from developing countries. New technologies enable a much more extensive automation of repetitive work in manufacturing but mass production systems are not able to produce the quality needed in the niche and affluent markets of Europe.

In the short term it is likely that this 'new' system and the Taylorist mass production system will both be used, as they focus on different markets. In the longer run, it seems that the Taylorist system will be increasingly automated or the products it manufactures will be produced almost exclusively in developing countries.

This change in the structure of manufacturing is altering the skills composition of employment, shifting demand from low skilled or motor skills to a skills mix involving more cognitive and inter-active, as well as more advanced, technological skills.

Firms that are surviving and succeeding in OECD countries are shifting from high volume production of standardised commodities to high value products serving the unique needs of particular customers. These are profitable because customers are willing to pay premium for goods and services that meet their needs exactly and because high value businesses cannot easily be duplicated by high volume competitors around the world. Businesses in advanced economies are moving to a higher ground based on specially tailored products and services. The new barrier to entry is not volume or price. It is skill in finding the right fit between particular technologies and particular markets. Many corporations no longer focus on products as such as their business strategies increasingly centre upon specialised knowledge.

18 – Jobs in the Future
Any forecasts of jobs in the future need to be located within

the context which recognises the very rapid changes which are taking place in the way work is being reorganised and new jobs are being invented. Our traditional methods of categorising jobs are unlikely to be very useful as guides to jobs in the 21st century, as they refer to forms of organising work which are unlikely to exist. Changes in the way work is organised are redefining many jobs, e.g., multi-skilling sometimes results in the amalgamation of several different categories of work.

Also new products, services and methods of organisation are resulting in large numbers of new jobs which cannot be defined, as they do not yet exist. The extensive nature of new job creation likely in the future can be seen in the projection that 80% of the products and services which will be traded in 10 years time do not yet exist.

Given this reservation in looking at future occupations using traditional categories, the growth in jobs in the 21st century is likely to be strongest in professional, technical, administrative and managerial occupations, weakest for agricultural, routine production and labouring and stable for low skilled services.

Within manufacturing, there will be an increase in skilled, technical and managerial positions and a decline in semi-skilled, and unskilled jobs and routine supervisory or managerial positions. Within services, the highest growth will be in higher qualification, higher income occupations with the biggest growth in health, social services, education, entertainment and in services to business. There will also be slower, but substantial, growth in relatively lower skilled, lower paid personal services work, e.g., restaurant, retail sales, cleaning. While the growth in low paying, insecure, low quality employment has been substantial, it has been slower than in higher skilled, higher income jobs.

The real problem in relation to unemployment is the lack of jobs which can be accessed at decent incomes by people with low skills or educational levels. In the short term, there are still likely to be significant numbers of people employed in routine production or data processing work. These jobs are likely to decline as the prices their standardised products

117

can command will be too low to provide decent wages because they will increasingly have to compete with Third World products, and also because they can be easily automated.

Occupations with the fastest Growth Rate and largest Job Gains and Losses

AUSTRALIA [1991–2001]

Fastest Growing
Psychologist, Social workers, Economists, Librarians, Mathematicians, statisticians, Actuaries, Veterinarians, Computing professionals, Speech pathologists, Welfare para-professionals, Accountants.

Largest Job Gains
Sales assistants, Managing supervisors, Numerical clerks, School teachers, Other labourers, Accountants, Computing professionals, Stenographers and Typists, Other salespersons, Registered nurses.

Largest Job losses or smallest Job Gains
Farmers, Farm managers, Agricultural labourers, Other social professionals, Stationary plant operators, Trade assistants, Other transport technicians, Other food trades, Metal Casing trades, Podiatrist, Other metal trades.

CANADA [1990–2000]

Fastest Growing
Child care workers, System analysts, Speech therapists, Sales occupations, Food and bev. prep. assistants, EDP equipment operators, Dental hygienists, Respiratory technicians, Auto fabrication, Veterinarians.

Largest Job Gains
Cashiers and tellers, System analysts, Sales managers, Chefs and Cooks, General managers, EDP equipment workers, Child care workers, Nurses, Sales clerks, salespersons, Secretaries, stenographers.

Largest Job Losses
Typists and Clerk-typists, Truck drivers, Commercial travellers, Fishing occupations, Telephone operators, Machine tool operators, Timber cutting, Paper production fab., Packaging occupations, Fish canning.

NETHERLANDS [1993–1998]

Fastest Growing
Journalists, Authors and Announcers, Physiotherapists and Occupational therapists, System analysts, Programme system supervisors, EEC technicians, Speech therapists and other Paramedical, Information service and Media specialists, Personnel officers, Vocational advisors, Registered nurses and Home Nursing personnel, Photographers, Film-makers, Designers, Window dressers, Visual and Performing Artists, Senior finance and sales managers, Physicians, Medical specialists, Pharmacists.

Largest Job Gains
Directors, Managers and Supervisors in manufacturing, Systems analysts, Programme and Systems supervisors, Registered nurses and Home Nursing personnel, Sales assistants, Senior finance and sales managers, Book-keepers, Bank and Tax department employees, Student nurses and Home Nursing personnel, Geriatric help, Kindergarten staff and nannies, Journalists, Authors and Announcers, Freight handlers, Packers and Packing workers.

Largest Job Losses
Shopkeepers, Retail and Wholesale staff, Primary and Special Education teachers, Building material, Glass and Ceramic production workers, Clothing, textile and fur product makers, Food and beverage processors, Upholsterers, Shoemakers and Leather workers, Agricultural workers, Carpenters and Woodworkers, Commercial representatives, Sales managers and Brokers, Electrical product assembly workers and Quality controllers, Welders and Engineering workers, Farmers.

UNITED STATES [1992–2005]

Fastest Growing
Home health aides, human service workers, Personal and Home Care aides, Computer engineers and Scientists, System analysts, Physical and corrective therapy assistants and aides, Physical therapists, Paralegals, Teachers, Special education, Medical assistants.

Largest Job Gains
Sales persons, retail, Registered nurses, Cashiers, General office clerk, Truck drivers, light and heavy, Waiters and Waitresses, Nursing aides, Orderlies and Attendants, Janitors and Cleaners, including Maid and Housekeeping cleaners, Food preparation workers, System analysts.

Largest Job Losses
Farmers, Sewing machine operators, garment, Cleaners and Servants, private household, Farmworkers, Typists and Word processors, Child care workers, private household, Computer operators, except peripheral equipment, Packaging and Filling machine oper-

ators and tenders, Inspectors, Testers and Graders, precision, Switchboard operators.

Source: Employment Outlook, OECD, 1994, pp. 88, 89, 90, 91.

CHAPTER VI

MAKING THE NEW WORLD WORK

1 – International Framework

During the 1950s and 1960s, most industrialised countries had full employment and, in many cases, a shortage of labour. From 1950–1973, the economies of the industrialised countries grew at an average of 5% per annum. The oil crisis in 1973 was followed by a halving of economic growth. This resulted from the drop in demand caused by the massive transfer of money to the oil producing countries and the rise in the costs of production due to the rise in energy prices.

The Breton Woods monetary system of stable exchange rates broke down at this time also, as did the social consensus on the distribution of the benefits of growth. Economic growth declined from 5–6% to 2–3% per annum. Since then there has been a slow growth in employment, a growth in unemployment in the EU and of low waged employment in the USA. There is now growing international concern about the growth in unemployment and low waged jobs and about the low rate of employment creation, particularly in the EU.

2 – Employment in Ireland

Employment in Ireland 1926 – 1994

		1,000s		
	Total	Agriculture	Industry	Services
1926	1205	652	159	395
1936	1229	613	201	415
1951	1211	496	280	435
1961	1040	379	259	406
1971	1045	273	323	449
1981	1124	189	366	569
1986	1081	178	310	615
1991	1121	165	320	636
1993	1146	144	312	690
1994	1155	141	314	700

Source: Central Statistics Office (Labour Force Survey).

Discussions on employment/unemployment in Ireland need to be located within the context of international economic developments. There is a growing recognition internationally that the problem of creating new employment and reducing unemployment, and low paid employment, must be given more urgent attention than in the past. There are deep-seated issues which have to be addressed which will not be solved by euphoric press statements or optimistic research reports of temporary improvements. As Jacques Delors put it, we must avoid 'conjunctual euphoria' with upswings in employment or economic figures. These are generally followed by downturns which wipe out the employment gains of the past. The downturn in the European economy in the 1990s wiped out the 10 million jobs which had been created in 1985–1990.

Employment/unemployment and economic growth patterns in Ireland have been broadly similar to the EU since 1980, with little growth in employment and also growing unemployment. Ireland has been the strongest growing economy in Europe in quite a few of these years and, ironically, has much higher than average unemployment. Japan, the USA and Scandinavian countries have had higher growth in employment and lower unemployment than countries in the EU.

Changes in employment 1987–1992
% Change per annum

	1987–1990	1991	1992	1993
Germany	1.8	2.6	–1.7	–2.4
UK	2.1	–3.2	–2.9	–1.2
France	1.1	0.1	–0.5	–1.0
US	1.6	–0.9	0.6	1.1
OECD	1.7	0.0	–0.1	–0.1
EC	1.7	0.3	–1.2	–1.7
Spain	3.2	0.2	–1.9	–4.6
Portugal	2.3	3.0	0.8	–1.5
Greece	0.9	–1.3	1.9	0.0
Ireland	**1.4**	**0.0**	**0.0**	**0.4**

Source: A Strategy for Competitiveness, Growth and Employment, NESC Report No. 96, 1993, p. 24.

Since 1970, the number of people at work in Ireland has increased by 100,000 approximately. From 1971–1981 the number increased by 80,000; from 1981–1987 the number declined; from 1987–1989 there was a strong growth in employment of 50,000. In the 1990s the number stabilised at roughly the same as in 1980. During this 25–year period, there have been substantial shifts in the sources of employment, with a large decline in agriculture and, more recently, in industry and the growth in services as the main source of employment.

GDP Growth
% Change per annum

	1986–1990	1991	1992	1993
Germany	3.4	3.7	2.0	–1.9
UK	3.0	–2.2	–0.6	1.8
France	3.2	0.7	1.3	–0.7
US	2.6	–1.2	2.1	2.6
OECD	3.3	0.7	1.5	1.2
EC	3.3	1.4	1.1	–0.4
Spain	4.8	2.3	1.0	–0.6
Portugal	4.7	2.2	1.4	0.6
Greece	1.7	1.8	1.4	1.1
Ireland (GNP)	**5.5**	**4.3**	**3.9**	**1.75**

Source: A Strategy for Competitiveness, Growth and Employment, NESC Report No. 96, 1993, p. 20.

Since 1960, the Irish economy has performed strongly relative to other European countries, achieving an average growth of 3.2% over the period. From 1973–1979 Ireland was the fastest growing country in the OECD; from 1982–1986 we had below average growth and since 1987 we have outperformed other OECD/EC countries.

The problem is that from the point of view of employment opportunities, all this increased growth in Ireland and Europe has not generated significant increases in employment or given low unemployment in Ireland or in the EU generally. As Dineen points out, in his article on employment in *Labour Market Review*, Ireland's GNP grew by 29% from 1980–1989, while numbers at work fell by 5.7%.

3 – Unemployment
In looking at unemployment in Ireland since 1960, we see it remained relatively stable at 5%–6% up until 1975. It has continued upwards since then with a few temporary de-

Unemployment Rate, Ireland and EC

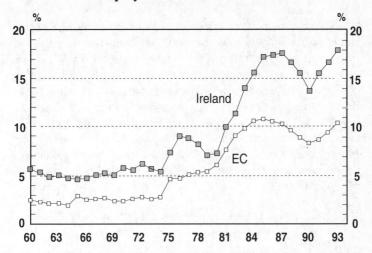

Source: 'Unemployment and Ecomonic Performance in Ireland: The Background' by Brendan Walsh in Labour Market Review, Volume 4, No. 2, FÁS, Winter 1993/94, p. 3.

clines, but each time from a higher level. It is now amongst the highest in OECD countries. As Professor Brendan Walsh points out, the trend is similar to the general pattern in the EU, but at much higher than average levels.

Rate of Employment

The rate of employment is an important element also, which needs to be considered when looking at the problem of employment/unemployment. The employment rate is a measure of the success or failure of any economy to create jobs. The employment rate is the ratio of the numbers employed to the population of working age. A low rate of employment means that a low percentage of those of working age are registered as part of the labour force. It means that there is a large number of people who, as well as those registered as unemployed, would be available potentially for work if it became available. This means that seeing the numbers of registered unemployed as the measure of the number of potential job seekers is not correct. With a low rate of participation, more people become available for work as the numbers of jobs increase.

This can result in no decrease in unemployment, despite the creation of new jobs. Seventy per cent of new employment goes to new entrants to the labour force, only 30% goes to unemployed. Raising the employment rate will require the creation of more new jobs than if the goal was simply reducing unemployment. The employment rate for Europe as a whole is lower than the USA or Japan with 58% in the EU compared to over 70% in Japan and the USA. The Irish employment rate is 51.5%. This low rate is primarily a reflection of the very low rate of participation by women in paid employment here.

Irish Population, Labour Force, and Labour Force Participation Rate 1980–1992

Year	Population	Population Aged 15+	Labour Force	LF participation rate
	(000)	(000)	(000)	(000)
1980	3,401	2,366	1,247	52.7
1981	3,443	2,400	1,272	53.0
1982	3,480	2,426	1,293	53.3
1983	3,504	2,462	1,307	53.1
1984	3,529	2,489	1,307	52.5
1985	3,540	2,506	1,305	52.1
1986	3,541	2,516	1,308	52.0
1987	3,546	2,533	1,312	51.8
1988	3,531	2,535	1,310	51.7
1989	3,510	2,535	1,292	51.0
1990	3,506	2,548	1,305	51.2
1991	3,526	2,582	1,334	51.7
1992	3,548	2,621	1,350	51.5

Source: A Strategy for Competitiveness, Growth and Employment, NESC, No. 96, 1993, p. 66.

4 – Backwards is not the Way Forward

Returning to nineteenth century economics and social organisation, as initiated by Ronald Reagan in the USA, was recognised by the speakers at the Centenary Conference as not the way forward. As a result of the United States Government removing social protection and investments in welfare, housing, education, health care and labour rights people in the USA had no choice (other than hunger and homelessness), but to accept any work on offer, whatever the rate of pay. Robert Reich, US Minister for Labour, points out that millions of jobs were created at wages below subsistence level and a whole new class of poor created. Much of the civil fabric of American society fell apart and wages for those already low paid declined further.

The social decline in the USA has become so pervasive that Francis Fukuyama, author of *The End of History*, said in a recent interview that 'the United States faces a crisis of associational life'. He says:

> the countries which have the most dynamic economies are those with the most vigorous networks of intermediate associations – Germany, Japan and, formerly, the USA. The art of associating is an important economic virtue, because it is an inherently flexible manner of facing challenges. People who trust each other and feel responsible to each other are good at adapting to new conditions. When all that is left of the rich texture of society is a contract between individuals, then America will be in real trouble. Undeniably, that is where we are headed. Not having enough economic choice is not our problem; our problem is the unravelling of the moral cohesion of societies.

Attempts at simplistic short term solutions through applying nineteenth century economic theory to 21st century economies is threatening the integration of civil society in the USA, and, to a lesser degree, in the UK and Europe. It is worth noting that in addition to the human suffering and social destruction which this policy has brought in the USA, it has not led to a higher rate of growth in the economy or in per capita income. As pointed out in an article by Frank Browne and Donal McGettigan in the FÁS *Labour Market Review* [volume 4, winter 1993/94], while growth in employment has been faster in the USA than in Europe, 1.8% as against 0.31% per annum, the growth in GDP has been slower in the USA, 2.9% compared to 3.2% per annum in Europe, and growth in GDP per capita was much slower, 1.8% in the USA compared to 2.7% per annum in Europe.

Since 1970, the USA has experienced constant and increasing poverty. The incidence of poverty in the USA is four times higher than in the EU. Sixty per cent of poor families in the USA have at least one member working but cannot earn enough to get above the poverty line. Fourteen per cent of the population is below the poverty threshold.

The challenge of employment is not just the creation of jobs at any price or of any kind. With no income or environmental standards there would be no problem in providing jobs for all. The full employment policy through slavery as practised in southern states of the USA or the policies of the former Soviet Union would be the perfect solution to unemployment. However, as Michael Porter of Harvard University points out the wealth of a country and the standard of living of people is not defined by the number of jobs in a country. 'It is the type of jobs, not just the ability to employ citizens at low wages, that is decisive for economic prosperity. The principal goal of a nation is to produce a high and rising standard of living for its citizens. If a nation loses its ability to compete in a range of high productivity/high wages industries its standard of living is threatened.'

The problem of employment/unemployment has come about, not because of a failure in the economies of Europe, but because of a slowness in recognising that the changes which are taking place in technologies, consumer tastes, global trade and the organisation of work are making many of the traditional theories and institutional infrastructures obsolete.

A new developmental infrastructure and changes in economic theory will be needed for the world of work of the 21st century. These will build on the advances which have been made in the growth of the productive capacity of the economy and in the fabric of civil society. Innovation is needed across the broad range of development strategies, locally, nationally and globally. A more urgent will is also needed to bring these changes about.

5 – More Economic Growth

To address the problem of unemployment and low rate of employment there must be an increase in the numbers in employment and in the levels of economic growth. Without increased economic growth the numbers in employment can only be expanded by reducing the living standards of those in work.

When we talk of the need for increased economic growth, it is important that we remind ourselves of the progress which has been made in the past 50 years particularly, and that even the modest rates of growth achieved over the past 25 years represent substantial expansion in the wealth of society. While the 2–3% growth rates averaged in European countries over the past 25 years is a lower percentage than in the 1950s and 1960s, it is still a rate that is very high by historical perspectives and is 3% of a much larger economy than existed in 1950. It is not 3% of the same amount. At 2% growth per year an economy doubles in size in 35 years, at 3% it doubles in 24 years.

The EU has set a target of reducing unemployment to 5% by the year 2000. The ILO outlines the growth needed to reduce unemployment in a number of countries to 5% by the year 2000. As can be seen in the chart on the next page this identifies the need for substantially higher levels of economic growth than most countries are achieving at present.

To achieve these higher levels of economic growth, a number of reforms are needed.

6 – Reform International Monetary System

At the core of the process of international economic development is the global monetary system. Instability in this system, as expressed in fluctuating currencies and exchange rates, spreads fear and uncertainty in relation to investment and the future. Confident planning for the future is undermined.

The creation of banking and the international monetary systems to facilitate investment was an important innovation in expanding the economic capacity of society. However, the recent emergence of the global financial markets which the

Forecasts of unemployment rates in the year 2000 (assuming that economic policies remain unchanged) and of growth required to reach a 5% unemployment rate in the year 2000

Country	GDP	Productivity	Employment	Active population	Unemployment rate in 2000	Required growth	Unemployment rate in 1995
USA	2.2	1.1	1.1	1.1	5.8	2.6	5.8
Japan	3.3	2.7	0.6	0.6	2.8	2.4	2.8
Germany	3.0	2.5	0.5	0.1	8.2	4.4	10.0
France	2.2	2.1	0.1	0.5	14.0	6.2	12.2
Italy	1.9	2.0	-0.1	0.2	13.2	5.6	11.9
UK	2.2	1.9	0.3	0.4	9.4	4.1	8.2
Spain	3.0	2.0	1.0	0.8	23.7	12.2	24.4
Portugal	3.0	2.1	0.9	0.6	5.5	3.2	6.9
Greece	2.5	1.4	1.1	0.2	6.9	3.4	11.0
Netherlands	2.0	1.2	0.8	0.2	6.8	2.8	9.5
Denmark	2.0	1.7	0.3	-0.2	8.2	3.4	10.5
Ireland	2.0	1.8	0.2	0.8	17.9	8.0	15.4
Belgium	2.0	1.8	0.2	0.0	11.8	5.1	12.7
Sweden	2.0	1.9	0.1	0.2	8.3	3.4	7.8
Norway	2.0	1.8	0.2	0.4	6.1	2.5	5.2
Switzerland	2.0	1.3	0.7	0.2	1.3	0.5	3.8
Finland	1.0	1.0	0.0	0.0	17.7	6.9	17.7
Austria	2.0	1.3	0.7	0.0	1.2	0.5	4.6
Iceland	2.0	1.0	1.0	0.8	5.3	2.1	6.2
Canada	2.0	1.0	1.0	1.3	11.5	4.9	10.2
Australia	2.0	0.9	1.1	1.6	11.7	5.0	9.5
New Zealand	2.0	1.5	0.5	0.8	9.5	4.0	8.1

Source: *World Employment, 1995, An ILO Report, 1995, p. 160.*

new technologies have made possible has fundamentally changed the structure of the international monetary system and the way it functions.

Information and communication technologies have made possible the global financial integration of exchanges in which $1000 billion per day is traded. These financial markets have no national boundaries or controls. This global flow of money is controlled, not by Governments, but by private institutions and individuals – banks, pension funds, private investors and trusts. This flow of money is growing rapidly and is altering the dynamics of global trade. Where formerly investment facilitated trade, it is becoming increasingly a reflection of the profits of speculation on itself, not an instrument of trade. The extent of the money involved is such that most Governments are powerless in relation to attacks on their currencies' values by speculative movements of money.

The value of national currencies can often be more a reflection of international speculative movements of currencies than the actual state of economies. Government budgetary policies are increasingly formed by the perceived threat of these speculators, rather than by the needs of society. Speculative movements in currency values and exchange rates can overnight alter the competitive position of companies and countries, and wipe out years of hard work, wage restraint and market development. *Employment in Europe* (1994) points out the significance of the movement of exchange rates in relation to countries' competitiveness:

> In general, it is exchange rate movements rather than differentials in productivity or wage rises which have been the major determinant of the cost competitiveness of European producers relative to those in the rest of the world, as well as between producers in different European countries. Exchange rate movements have been far from smooth, however, and rates have fluctuated wildly over the past 10–15 years, causing equally wide swings in relative costs of production and almost certainly damaging world trade, economic growth and employment.

The creation of an international mechanism to bring stability and democratic control to the international speculative movement of

131

currencies is the most urgent modernisation reform needed for the creation of an effective infrastructure for employment and general social and economic development for the 21st century. Achieving this goal will require a greater degree of co-operation and inter-governmental solidarity in economic policies. It will involve the new kind of balance of co-operation and competitiveness which is taking place between companies in the networking form of development which is emerging globally. Actively promoting this international mechanism should be a part of our employment development strategies. There needs to be a clear recognition that the instability caused by these speculative monies results in raising interest rates and slowing down job creation and economic growth. The question of taxing these speculative flows of monies should also be investigated urgently.

7 – Promote Open World Trade

Total world output has grown more since World War II than in the whole of human history before that. Growth in world trade has been a central dynamic of this achievement. Total world output has grown by 3% per annum since 1950; 1950–1960 by 5%, 1961–1973 by 0.5%, 3.5% in 1974–1980, and 3.3% in the 1980s. It fell to 1.1% in the 1990s recession. With recovery now underway, it is projected to return to the 3% range which has been the norm since the 1970s. In 1990, total world output was double what it had been in 1970. The growth rates since the 1950s have exceeded population growth, giving a steady increase in global output per head. Real per capita output was 26% higher. There has been considerable global economic progress. How this progress has been divided between and within countries varies considerably.

A major reason for the advances which have been made in standards of living globally has been the growth of international trade. The growth in developing economies now occurring offers the possibility of increasing growth rates in developed economies due to the demand for goods and services it will potentially generate. World trade is projected to grow by 20% as a result of the GATT Agreement. While the increased trade may result in a loss of markets for some of the traditional industries in developed countries, we should resist any drives to protectionism and the closing off of trade. If it is necessary to slow down the process of adaptation of the economy, subsidisation on a short term basis is more desirable and less costly than barriers to trade. Positive adjustment actions are more desirable than any defensive measures.

The most effective means of supporting employment and adjusting to changes in global trade are

a) informed and long term planning based on growing and declining sources of employment

b) education, training and upskilling of the workforce and,

c) continuous innovation in products and processes.

Actively opening up trade with developing economies should be part of our strategies for employment.

8 – Loosen the Purse Strings

> We are suffering, not from the rheumatics of old age, but from the growing pains of over rapid changes, from the painfulness of readjustment between one economic period and another. The increase of technical efficiency has been taking place faster than we can deal with the problem of labour absorption; the improvement in the standard of life has been a little too quick; the banking and monetary system of the world has been preventing the rate of interest from falling as fast as equilibrium requires.
>
> J. M. KEYNES

Since the late 1970s the economic, monetary and fiscal policies of Governments in Europe have been largely defined by the European Monetary System. The Maastricht Treaty defines the criteria to which Governments must conform, in the move towards creating a single currency. These criteria see inflation kept within the limits of 2% above the average of the three countries with the lowest inflation, public deficit less than 3% of GDP and public debt not exceeding 60% of GDP. German interest rates have been the primary determinant of European interest rates. The near hyper inflation of the late 1970s after the oil embargo and also the German reunification of 1989, have both reinforced a deep concern with inflation.

The restrictive monetary policies which have been followed in Europe have resulted in relatively slow and erratic growth. The expansion in the late 1980s which followed relaxation of monetary policies brought very substantial increases in jobs in Europe but the high interest rates in early 1990s caused a slowdown which wiped out the equivalent of the 10 million jobs which had been created.

Professor Kenneth Galbraith feels that we have created what he calls a 'culture of contentment' in which the 80% in employment are doing very well while 20% are excluded from the benefits of the growing economy, either by unemployment in Europe or low pay work in the USA. The 2–3% growth in the developed economies, while being slow in comparison to earlier periods, is still substantial and gives comfortable rises in standards of living to those in work.

Professor Galbraith rejects the views of free market economists who argue that by removing restrictions in the market, the economy would absorb all the unemployed. Their thinking ignores the advances which have been made in the productive capacity of modern economies. These economies can produce all the needed goods and services without needing all the potential labour. For example, the EU produces 25% of the world's GDP, involving 60% of the EU's potential labour force. Economies can stabilise around high levels of unemployment and active stimulation of demand by Governments may be needed to shift this threshold.

J. K. Galbraith says:

> In substantial measure, though the matter is never put quite so bluntly, modern economic policy in all industrial countries makes unemployment the instrument for achieving price stability. Too great a decline in unemployment, too close an approach to full employment, it is held, brings the threat of inflation. In the modern social structure the world of relatively fixed incomes, pensioners, a large rentier class and the highly influential financial community inflation is more feared than unemployment. That is suffered by someone else. It is quite possible we should accept a regime of modest price increases as alternatives to unemployment. Better that than the waste, the social cost, of idleness.

Dr Cornell, OECD, and Michael Hansenne, ILO, both point out that there is an argument for stimulation. Michael Hansenne said: 'Every social system, Government, employers, central banks, and the labour movement has to decide the right amounts, the non-dangerous amount within their own national economic context. But nobody can deny that there is some amount of slack in many places that could be taken up by more stimulated policies'.

This stimulation, they felt, should come through changes in monetary policies. There did not seem to be much room in fiscal policies, as most Governments have large budget deficits since the oil shock of 1974–1979. The process of reflation needs to be co-ordinated internationally as any one country attempting to do so on its own would risk developing budget deficits and attacks from international speculators on its exchange rate.

9 – Increase Employment Intensity of Growth

As well as increasing economic growth there is a need to increase the employment intensity of growth. The employment intensity of growth is the term used to describe the relative amount of employment that economic growth generates. The employment intensity of growth is a vital determinant of the levels of employment created. In the classical economic thinking, which pervades our employment strategies, a central assumption is that there is an automatic and determined relationship between levels of economic growth, the amount of employment generated, and the decline in unemployment. The assumption here is that the faster the economy grows the more jobs are created and the lower unemployment will be. These assumptions do not reflect the way modern economies or societies function.

The levels of employment which rates of growth generate are not determined by 'the economy', by some divine law or by mathematical formula. Similar levels of growth generate very different levels of employment and unemployment in different countries. The level of employment generated by levels of growth are the result of choices which a society makes about the pattern of economic activities through which it generates growth and also the way it chooses to distribute the benefits of growth. As Michael Hansenne, ILO, points out:

> Employment problems are not predetermined outcomes of the working of uncontrollable forces, such as globalisation, intensified competition and technological change. They are the result of social choice; commissions or omissions in economic and social policies and shortcomings in institutional arrangements. The proof of this lies in the fact that countries at similar levels of development and subject to the same economic forces, have achieved widely different employment outcomes.

The levels of employment generated by similar levels of economic growth varies considerably between different countries as can be seen from the diagram below. Similarly, the levels of economic growth have not been the decisive factor in the levels of unemployment or rates of employment in different countries.

Economic Growth and Employment, 1970–1993

	Growth in Ecnomy	Growth in Employment
USA	70%	49%
EU	81%	9%
Japan	173%	25%
Spain	103%	–0.3%
Ireland	**100%**	**9%**
Germany	70%	11%
France	77%	6%
Italy	85%	18%
UK	51%	3%

Source: European Union White Paper on Growth, Competitiveness and Employment, 1993, p. 125.

Some countries, like Switzerland, Japan, Austria, Sweden and the USA, all had very low levels of unemployment, with medium levels of economic growth, while others like Spain and Ireland had high levels of unemployment with similar or higher levels of growth.

The pattern of activities through which growth is created, as well as the way growth is distributed, are important determinants of the amount of employment which levels of growth generate. By international standards, Ireland has a low level of employment creation relative to levels of economic growth.

Initiatives required to increase the employment intensity of economic growth will include:

(i) Reform Taxation System
The taxation system needs to evolve to reflect the evolution of the economy and promote more jobs intensive growth.

a) Reduce Social Costs of Employment
Throughout OECD countries, there is acceptance by Governments of the need to shift the focus of taxation off labour as a means of increasing the employment content of the economy. The aim is to increase the attractiveness of employing people and to make it more worthwhile for people to take up employment, particularly lower paid employment. It is both inefficient and unjust that the low paying jobs carry a heavy burden of taxation and social costs.

The EU White Paper recommends 'in order to help maintain employment and create new jobs without reducing wage levels steps should be taken to reduce non-wage costs, particularly for less skilled labour. Non-wage costs bear relatively more heavily on those in low paid employment. Member States should set themselves the target of reducing non-wage labour costs by an amount equivalent to 1% to 2% of GDP. This reduction should apply as a priority to the lowest earning'.

137

Statutory charges on labour (approximation used: personal income taxes and social security contributions)

Country	1970	1991	Change 1970–1991 *(as % of GDP)*
Belgium	19.6	29.5	9.9
Denmark	21.2	27.3	6.1
Germany	18.8	25.9	7.1
Greece	10.1	16.5	6.4
Spain	8.2	20.4	12.2
France	16.9	25.4	8.5
Ireland	**8.3**	**17.8**	**9.5**
Italy	12.7	23.6	10.9
Luxembourg	16.2	25.0	8.8
Netherlands	22.7	29.9	7.0
Portugal	–	16.0	–
UK	16.7	16.7	0.0
EUR	16.6	23.5	6.9
USA	15.9	19.4	3.5
Japan	8.6	17.6	9.0

Source: European Union White Paper on Growth, Competitiveness and Employment, 1993, p. 136.

b) Shift Burden of Taxation
The loss of revenue from reducing taxation and social charges on employment, particularly low waged work, could be replaced by shifting taxation to other parts of the economy through new taxes.

1. Tax on Financial Dealing
This is a most obvious tax to reflect the evolution of the economy. As pointed out earlier, financial dealing is now the largest industry in money terms, affecting the whole structure of employment and economies, yet it is not taxed. Effective taxation of these activities could be a major source of revenue to fund public services to meet the change in needs, e.g., care of the elderly.

2. Tax on Energy
This would cut down on CO_2 pollution and encourage environmentally friendly technologies and products.

3. Tax on Units of Output

The growing automation of production needs to be reflected in taxation. New ways need to be developed to enable public services to benefit from increased production – taxation on units of output would achieve this. It is a tax on capital rather than on employment.

(ii) Invest in People

As well as making it more attractive to hire people, there should also be positive support to encourage investment in people. Individuals and companies should be enabled to charge education and training expenditure against tax. The skills levels of the workforce could be counted in the assets of companies.

The EU White Paper on *Growth, Competitiveness and Jobs* advocates changing Government investment strategies from supporting capital investment in firms to supporting investment in the 'intangibles' of 'organisational capacity', which is where most value added is now created, and most employment opportunities lie. This means investing in skills like research, marketing, inter-personal communications, particularly co-operative and value adding communication skills, team working, abstract thinking and skills in information technology.

The White Paper states:

> Government policies must, in future, accord at least the same priority to knowledge based investment as they do to physical investment. This type of investment is becoming the key element in bringing about growth that is durable, creates skilled jobs, and is economical in its use of resources. There should be a review of the criteria governing admissibility of aid to industry, which tends to encourage firms to increase capital intensity of production and boost their physical as opposed to non-physical investment.

Since workforce skills are now a decisive factor in determining the employment generating capacity of a society, investment in education and training are vital components in creating labour intensive growth. Government policies in relation to taxation, company accounting and grant aids should reflect and encourage this. Aids to industry should include criteria on the levels of ongoing training being undertaken by companies.

(iii) Reduce Working Time
Increasing the labour intensity of growth can also be helped by reducing the length of the working week and overall working life so that more people share the work available. It is also a means of generating more demand and increasing economic growth. The reduction in working time and work sharing becomes easier as societies become more productive and more affluent. People are able to access a higher level of living standards and free time becomes a significant part of their general self fulfilment. The growing prosperity in Ireland and Europe in the future will create more favourable conditions for achieving shorter working time. Income per head is projected to grow 30% over the next 15 years.

A variety of options for reducing working time are being explored in the EU, including various forms of educational, parental and sabbatical leave and the introduction of monthly or annual working hours. The Netherlands has gone furthest in reducing working time – those in employment work an average of 33 hours a week; Denmark is also low at 35 hours.

10 – Long-Term Unemployment

Technology both eliminates jobs and creates jobs. Generally it destroys lower wage, lower productivity jobs, while it creates jobs that are more productive, high-skill and better paid. Historically, the income-generating effects of new technologies have proved more powerful than the labour-displacing effects; technological progress has been accompanied not only by higher output and productivity, but also by higher overall employment. The transition from old to new technologies is a demanding process that can create mismatches between the skills that people have and those that are needed. The workers who lose their jobs and are not able to take up the new opportunities tend to remain unemployed for long periods. The gap between the workers who benefit from technological change and those who lose from it risks becoming socially divisive.

OECD Science and Technology Review, 1993

There is a very deep transition taking place in the jobs market in Ireland, and in developed economies generally. The skills level of jobs is rising and there is a rapid decline in unskilled and semi-skilled jobs. This is particularly the situation for blue collar work for men. Technological advancement is resulting in skills obsolescence and deskilling. This has been most pervasive in manufacturing but commentators are predicting a similar pattern in white collar work ranging from data processing and routine supervisory and managerial roles.

The result of this process is the growth of numbers of people who are long-term unemployed, and effectively unskilled in relation to the jobs market. There is also an increase in the number of people looking for the lower skilled work. In some countries this is creating an increasing divide in incomes between lower skilled and other work.

The traditional idea that expansion in employment will automatically re-absorb the unemployed will not work in the future. People who are long-term unemployed will not be able to access the new jobs as they will not have the education and skills needed. The majority of long-term unemployed have low levels of formal education. In their article, in *Labour Market Review* [volume 5, winter 1994], John Fitzgerald and Gerard Hughes of the ESRI predict that while there will be ample job opportunities for people with skills in the year 2000, there will still be 200,000 unemployed who will not be able to access these jobs, due to lack of skills or education. The jobs becoming available in the traded goods sector of the economy will increasingly have a high knowledge and high skill content and will not be accessible to people who are long-term unemployed.

Growth in real wages of low-paid workers

Annualised percentage change

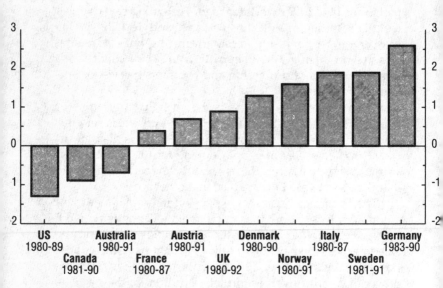

US 1980-89	Australia 1980-91	Austria 1980-91	Denmark 1980-90	Italy 1980-87	Germany 1983-90
Canada 1981-90	France 1980-87	UK 1980-92	Norway 1980-91	Sweden 1981-91	

There were contrasting trends in the dispersion of wages, between low-skilled and high-skilled workers. In the English-speaking countries, wage differentials widened over the 1980s. In the continental European countries on the other hand, wage differentials were either broadly unchanged or increased only slightly after narrowing decades earlier.

The widening of the wage differentials was associated with actual falls of real wages for low-skilled male workers in Australia, Canada and, especially, in the United States. The United Kingdom, however experienced both a sharp increase in earnings inequality and increases in real wages of the low-skilled, because of the rapid growth of wages in general in the 1980s.

Source: The OECD Jobs Study: Facts, Analysis, Strategies, 1994, p. 22.

Total unemployment rate and incidence of long-term unemployment (LTU)

	1979		1985		1989		1990		1991	
	Unemployment rate	LTU incidence	Unemployment rate	LTU incidence	Unemployment rate	LTU incidence	Unemployment rate	LTU incidence	Unemployment rate	LTU incidence
Australia	6.2	18.1	8.2	30.9	6.1	23.0	6.9	21.6	9.6	24.9
Belgium	7.5	61.5	12.3	69.8	9.3	76.3	8.7	69.9	9.3	–
Canada	7.4	3.4	10.5	10.3	7.5	6.8	8.1	5.7	10.3	7.2
Denmark	6.2	36.2	9.0	39.3	9.3	25.9	9.5	33.7	10.4	–
Finland	6.0	–	5.0	21.1	3.5	6.9	3.5	–	7.6	–
France	6.0	30.3	10.2	46.8	9.4	43.9	8.9	38.3	9.4	37.3
Germany	2.9	28.7	7.1	47.9	5.6	49.0	4.9	46.3	4.3	–
Greece	1.9	–	7.8	46.2	7.4	52.4	7.0	51.7	8.2	–
Ireland	**7.1**	**38.2**	**17.4**	**64.7**	**15.6**	**67.3**	**13.7**	**67.2**	**15.8**	–
Italy	7.8	51.2	10.2	65.8	12.1	70.4	11.1	71.1	11.0	–
Japan	2.1	16.8	2.6	13.1	2.3	18.7	2.1	19.1	2.1	17.9
Netherlands	3.5	35.9	10.0	60.7	7.4	49.9	6.4	48.4	5.9	–
New Zealand	1.9	–	3.6	–	7.2	14.7	7.8	18.6	10.3	21.2
Norway	1.9	2.9	2.6	10.2	4.9	11.6	5.2	19.2	5.5	20.2
Portugal	8.2	–	8.7	–	5.0	48.3	4.7	48.1	4.1	–
Spain	8.6	29.5	21.5	56.7	17.3	58.5	16.3	54.0	16.3	51.1
Sweden	1.7	6.8	2.4	11.4	1.4	6.5	1.5	4.8	2.7	–
UK	4.5	29.5	11.6	48.6	6.2	40.8	5.9	36.1	8.3	–
USA	5.8	4.2	7.2	9.5	5.3	5.7	5.5	5.6	6.7	6.3

Source: Employment Outlook, OECD, 1993, p. 87.

143

Irish educational qualifications of those at work and unemployed, 1991

Educational level	At work	Unemployed	Short-term unemployed	Long-term Total
No qualification	2.4	40.1	24.3	47.2
Intermediate/ Group Cert	25.6	34.5	37.7	33.2
Leaving Cert	30.9	18.6	26.9	14.9
3rd Level	20.8	6.7	11.1	4.8
Total	100.0	100.0	100.0	100.0

Source: A Strategy for Competitivenes, Growth and Employment, No. 96, NESC, 1993, p. 479.

Significant new investment will be needed to absorb the long-term unemployed back into the labour force and to prevent the further build up of long-term unemployed. It is necessary to decrease the inflow into unemployment and increase the outflow. As can be seen from the next table there is a very low outflow from unemployment in Ireland. In Ireland over 65% of unemployed have been unemployed for over 12 months. Creating new jobs does not necessarily bring a reduction in unemployment or long-term unemployed.

Decreasing the inflow into unemployment will involve more pro-active training of people in work, as well as those outside work, to equip them to access new jobs and absorb new technologies. Public expenditure could be used to develop employment opportunities for low skilled work in the non-traded sectors of the economy. Public employment contracts could be used to discriminate in favour of long-term unemployed and public projects focused on this type of work. In many cases, people who are long-term unemployed are concentrated in particular geographical areas. Specific investments to generate employment can be focused on these areas. The locally based initiatives under the various national programmes provide a vehicle to mobilise local resources and target local needs.

There is a paradox at the core of modern economies

144

Employment rates and turnover of the pool of unemployed, 1991

Country	Employment rate	Monthly outflow rate	Monthly inflow rate	Estimated average duration unemployment (months)
United States	70.5	37.3	2.1	2.5
Sweden	83.3	30.0	0.4	3.8
Canada	67.8	23.8	2.3	3.7
Japan	73.6	23.6	0.3	5.0
Norway	72.8	20.6	0.9	4.7
UK	71.5	13.4	0.6	8.7
Australia	66.9	11.1	1.0	7.6
Denmark	74.1	8.3	0.7	17.0
Germany	64.8	8.0	0.2	14.2
Netherlands	61.7	5.6	0.1	19.5
France	60.2	5.5	0.3	22.5
Belgium	57.1	5.1	0.3	23.3
Ireland	**52.4**	**4.2**	**0.3**	**29.2**
Italy	54.3	3.3	0.2	38.9
Spain	48.0	2.0	0.2	42.3

Source: The OECD Jobs Study, Evidence and Explanations, Part II, The Adjustment Potential of the Labour Market, 1994, p. 89.

which will continue in the next century – we want to generate increased employment, while at the same time the thrust of the modernisation process is the drive to increase the output per person and thereby increase productivity, which reduces the need for people. If a country is not raising productivity and skills levels, then it will lose markets and employment. The goods and services which are in growth sectors in OECD countries are increasingly high technology, high-skill based. These activities do not provide employment for people with lower skills. Some countries have been more successful than others in dealing with this problem.

Three different strategies have been used to deal with low skills and long-term unemployment. The USA solution has been to remove social protections and decrease wages for lower paid, low skilled work. This has expanded the numbers of low paid jobs, reduced unemployment and created very wide disparities of income. It still has left unemployment at 7% in the USA.

Austria, Sweden, Norway and Japan have maintained very low rates of unemployment (1.5%–2%) since the 1950s without lowering wages and maintaining reasonable equality of income distribution. Even in a very severe recession recently, Japan has maintained this low level of unemployment. All of these countries have a sector of the economy which is not judged by market forces. Austria, Sweden and Norway use the public sector to keep unemployment low and provide jobs for the less skilled and less qualified. Less skilled jobs contract most in periods of economic downturn. Higher skilled jobs have continued to expand in recent downturns. Japan uses a different strategy than the other countries, as Paul Ormerod points out.

While Japanese industry is notoriously efficient and focused on productivity in its internationally traded sectors, the domestic sector is not subject to this pressure and employs far more people than similar services in Europe, e.g., tourism, catering, bars, etc. Unlike in the USA model, people in these jobs are paid decent wages. The result is a well paid, lower productivity, expensive domestic traded services sector. Austria and Sweden pay for this employment through higher taxes on wages and profits. The Japanese pay through higher consumption costs for expensive services.

The social cohesion which these systems create are a powerful motivation rather than the opposite, as those wishing to return to nineteenth century economies would proclaim. The Japanese economy has outperformed every economy over the past 20 years. Austria and Sweden enjoy standards of living among the highest in the world and have had growth rates similar to EU averages. Economies like Austria, Sweden, Germany, and Japan, which also have relatively narrow disparities of earnings, perform better in the longer run than those driven by gross disparities of income, like the US or the UK.

The challenge of funding this employment of less skilled or less market defined jobs involves having a highly successful internationally traded sector, which gives high return on investment and high wages. This can generate income or taxes to subsidise the other sector. Ireland, unfortunately, has not yet developed this economic capacity. The goods and services which are growth sectors in OECD countries are increasingly high tech, with a high knowledge content. Irish industry is still predominantly in the low tech sector.

Structure of Irish-owned Industry 1983 and 1990

% Total Irish-owned Industry

	Employment		Net Output	
	1983	1990	1983	1990
High-tech	3.7	6.4	3.5	5.6
Medium-tech	14.6	18.3	13.1	18.7
Low-tech	81.7	75.3	83.4	75.6
Total Irish Owned	100.0	100.0	100.0	100.0

Source: A Strategy for Competitiveness, Growth and Employment, No. 96, NESC, 1993, p. 255.

11 – Beyond Welfare

The creation of the social welfare system was a major social advance. It provides a basic guarantee of minimum entitlements which come with citizenship. It was an expression both of a European commitment to social justice and solidarity, and of the growth in the productive capacity of the economy. There is a growing view that the way these benefits operate needs changing, as Dr Cornell, OECD, expressed it, 'to make them more employment supportive, not to reduce protection'. We need to move them from being desperate redistributive measures to being supportive of creativity.

When unemployment benefits developed, they were seen as temporary support in helping people with the transition between a plentiful supply of full-time jobs. They were never meant as being adequate for a permanent way of living. For many people, they have become the source of permanent income, due to the growth of unemployment, particularly long-term unemployment. A serious question must be asked as to whether this is an acceptable situation for the future, Present realistic projections on economic growth and employment are that there will be a sizeable percentage of people in Ireland unemployed into the 21st century, living long-term on unemployment benefits. This system and its relationship to the labour market needs to be overhauled.

12 – Losing Old Jobs, Creating New Ones
In thinking about increasing employment we need to keep job losses, as well as job creation, as part of the picture. The fact that the number in employment has not increased significantly in Ireland or Europe over the past 15 years does not mean that no new jobs were created. Increased numbers in employment are a reflection of how much job creation exceeds job loss. As pointed out earlier, a significant rate of job loss is an inherent part of the process of economic development. One in ten jobs is lost each year in OECD countries. This is happening in all economies, but occurs particularly rapidly in economies like Ireland which have a big percentage of people in agriculture or labour intensive industries. Both of these are rapidly declining sources of employment in developed economies.

The disappearance of jobs cannot be understood within the context of economic slowdowns only but must also be seen as part of the rapid transition of the economy now under way globally. Employment policies need to be framed within this context of the continuous upgrading and transformation of the sources of employment. There needs to be much more attention given to identifying areas in decline and remedial action taken to upskill workers and upgrade products. We must agree on more efficient and just ways of managing transition than using unemployment as the means of managing change.

Due to the rapidity of technical and product obsolescence, the generation of new skills and new activities which will provide employment needs to be a part of every organisation's agenda. For workers this is very important if their long-term employability and work is to be secure. This will involve substantial changes in management of decision-making in companies. All the potential creativity of the workforce needs to be involved in innovation. This assumes a culture which reflects the creativity of workers and reflects

Job gains and job losses
Average annual rate as a % of total employment

	Canada	Denmark	Finland	France	Germany	Italy	New Zealand	Sweden	UK	USA
	1983–91	1983–89		1984–92	1983–90	1984–92	1987–92	1985–92	1985–91	1984–91
Gross job gains	**14.5**	**16.0**	**10.4**	**13.9**	**9.0**	**12.3**	**15.7**	**14.5**	**8.7**	**13.0**
Openings	3.2	6.1	3.9	7.2	2.5	3.9	7.4	6.5	2.7	8.4
Expansions	11.2	9.9	6.5	6.7	6.5	8.4	8.3	8.0	6.0	4.6
Gross job losses	**11.9**	**13.8**	**12.0**	**13.2**	**7.5**	**11.1**	**19.8**	**14.6**	**6.6**	**10.4**
Closures	3.1	5.0	3.4	7.0	1.9	3.8	8.5	5.0	3.9	7.3
Contractions	8.8	8.8	8.7	6.3	5.6	7.3	11.3	9.6	2.7	3.1
Net employment change	**2.6**	**2.2**	**-1.6**	**0.6**	**1.5**	**1.3**	**-4.1**	**-0.1**	**2.1**	**2.6**
Net entry (openings less closures)	0.2	1.1	0.5	0.2	0.5	0.2	-1.1	1.5	-1.2	1.1
Net expansion (expansions less contractions)	2.4	1.1	-2.1	0.4	0.9	1.1	-3.0	-1.6	3.4	1.5
Job turnover	**26.3**	**29.8**	**22.4**	**27.1**	**16.5**	**23.4**	**35.5**	**29.1**	**15.3**	**23.4**

Source: Employment Outlook, OECD, 1994, p. 106.

this in the decision-making process, by involving workers and their unions actively in all the decision-making of the company. The Japanese have demonstrated the effectiveness of workforce involvement in their economic success over the past 50 years.

The knowledge creating company which will survive and grow in the future will be managed in a way which involves, develops and respects the intelligence and commitment of the workforce as the source of wealth. This will require a profound culture changes in our traditional Anglo/ US style of management. Our achievements in the next century will depend to a large degree on our success in making this change.

A Japanese Viewpoint: Why the West will Lose

We are going to win and the industrial west is going to lose; there is nothing much you can do about that, because the reasons for your failure are within yourselves.

Your firms are built on the Taylor model; even worse, so are your heads. With your bosses doing the thinking, while the workers wield the screwdrivers, you are convinced deep down that this is the right way to run a business.

For you, the essence of management is getting the ideas out of the heads of the bosses and into the hands of labour.

We are beyond the Taylor model; business, we know, is now so complex and difficult, the survival of firms so hazardous in an environment increasingly unpredictable, competitive, and fraught with danger, that their continued existence depends on the day-to-day mobilisation of every ounce of intelligence.

For us, the core of management is precisely this art of mobilising and putting together the intellectual resources of all employees in the service of the firm. Because we have measured better that you the scope of new technologies and economic challenges, we know that the intelligence of a handful of technocrats, however brilliant and smart they may be, is no longer enough for a real chance of success.

Only by drawing on the combined brain power of all its employees can a firm face up to the turbulence and constraints of today's environment.

That is why our large companies give their employees three to four times more training than yours, this is why they seek constantly everybody's suggestions and why they demand from the educational system increasing numbers of graduates as well as bright and well-educated generalists, because these people are the lifeblood of industry ....

K. Matsushita [Matsushita Electrical Industrial Company,
Japan]

13 – A Century of Creativity

While macro-economic policies are important in relation to employment creation, at the core of the job creating process is the human imagination and will. In its essence, job creation is a human process which is driven by the imagination, will and commitment of people, to individually and collectively find new and better ways of meeting changing human needs and improving the experience of human life.

Generating jobs which improve the standard of living is not just a matter of buying machines or reforming structures. It involves the generation of a spirit of innovation throughout a culture which motivates people to actively search for better ways of meeting individual and social needs. Without the imagination and involvement of people all the structural and technical changes in the world will not generate employment which improves the standard of living.

The creation of this innovative society will require a profound change in Irish society; moving from a culture permeated by fatalism, dependency and conformity to one permeated by a valuing of individual and collective creativity, diversity, conviviality and quality. Employment creation is a social process which reflects the culture of a society and grows out of the creativity of people.

AFTERWORD

I was commissioned by Congress to write this book. For that I am very grateful, particularly to Peter Cassells and Oliver Donohoe who also gave inspiration and constructive feedback, which always resulted in more work. At one stage, it seemed like this could go on forever. However, finally it came together in a way which seemed to suit all.

The book is a book of hope and confidence in the continued uplifting of the quality of life for a growing percentage of people globally and nationally. For Ireland, as a part of an increasingly affluent European society, there is the possibility of very significant improvements in standards of living and work opportunities. Seeking out change, understanding its messages and responding spontaneously and innovatively to the challenges and opportunities it offers, are the kind of attitudes we need to develop to function effectively in this rapidly changing society. The traditional attitudes of seeing change as a threat will not help to actively participate in the creation of the future.

Innovations in technologies, work practices and products will require lifelong learning and relearning about technologies, skills, ways of working and relating. A huge diversity of new job opportunities will emerge. These will generally be of higher quality and wage levels that at present. The work environment will be transformed for the better, as employers are faced with the need to evoke the innovative commitment of the workforce and also to meet the working needs of the much more highly educated workforce. While the standard of living will continue to rise with growing shortages of people for many new jobs, there is also an increasing tendency towards exclusion of a sizeable percentage of people from this new work and growing wealth. There will be an ongoing need for very active social intervention by Governments to prevent this happening. A new sense of inter-personal solidarity will need to penetrate our society at all levels.

While this book has pointed out some of the likely trends in the 21st century, there will no doubt be many changes which none of us can predict. If the book stimulates you to open up to new possibilities it will have been worthwhile. I also hope it gives you some enjoyment.

We are not passive recipients of the future. It is available to be shaped and created. The real challenge of the future is a challenge to our ability to individually and collectively co-create and improve our world.

PADDY WALLEY
JUNE 1995

FURTHER READING

Bateson, Gregory, *Steps to an Ecology of Mind*, Chandler Publishing Company.

Beer, Stafford, *Platform for Change*, John Wiley.

Costello, M., and Aoyama, Y., 'Paths towards the informational Society', *International Labour Review*, Vol. 133, No. 1.

Drucker, Peter, *Managing the Future*, Butterworth Heiman Ltd.

Fisher, Roger & Ury, William, *Getting to Yes*, Arrow Books Ltd.

Freeman, Chris & Bengt–AKE, Lungrall, *Small Countries Facing the Technological Revolution*, Pinter.

Freeman, Chris, *Technology and Economic Performance – Lessons from Japan*, Pinter.

Galbraith, John Kenneth, *The Culture of Contentment*, Sinclair Stevenson.

Galbraith, John Kenneth, *The World Economy since the War*, Sinclair Stevenson.

Gardiner, Howard, *Frames of Mind*, Basic Books/Harper Collins.

Gardiner, Howard, *Multiple Intelligences – the Theory in Practice*, Basic Books/Harper Collins.

Gorz, Andre, *Critique of Economic Reason*, Verso.

Hamel, Gary & Prahalad, C. K., *Competing for the Future*, Harvard Business School Publishing Corporation.

Handy, Charles, *The Future of Work*, Basic Blackwell.

Howard, Richard, *The Learning Imperative*, Harvard Business School Publishing Corporation.

Keane, Colm, *The Jobs Crisis*, RTE/Mercier Press.

Kennedy, Paul, *Preparing for the 21st Century*, Fontana.

Leadbetter, Charles & Lloyd, John, *In Search of Work*, Pelican.

Lipnack, Jessica & Stamps, Jeffrey, *The Teamnet Factor*, Oliver Wright Publications.

Luboff, Shoshana, *In the Age of the Smart Machine*, Heiman Professional Publishing Ltd.

Nyhan, Barry, *Developing People's Ability to Learn*, European Inter-Varsity Press.

Osmerod, Paul, *The Death of Economics*, Faber and Faber.

Pascale, Richard, *Managing on the Edge*, Penguin.

Porter, Michael E., *The Competitive Advantage of Nations*, Free Press.

Quinn, James, B., *Intelligent Enterprise*, Free Press.

Ray, Michael & Ritmaler, Alan, *The New Paradigm in Business*, Putnam Publishing Group.

Reich, Robert, *The Work of Nations*, Vintage/Random House.

Veal, A. J., *Leisure and the Future*, Allen and Unwin.

Walley, Paddy, *Learning the Future*, Meitheal Mhuigheo/Galway VEC.

Watzlawick, Paul, Barclay, Janet B., Jackson, Dan, *Pragmatics of Human Communication*, W. V. Norton and Company.

Wonack, James T., Jones, Daniel, Ross, David, *The Machine that Changed the World*, Maxwell Macmillan International.

LIST OF ABBREVIATIONS

EU	European Union/European Comission [Brussels]
GATT	General Agreement on Tariffs and Trade
GDP	Gross Domestic Product
ICTU	Irish Congress of Trade Unions
ILO	International Labour Organisation [Geneva]
NESC	National Economic and Social Council [Dublin]
OECD	Organisation for Economic Co-operation and Delevopment [Paris]

LIST OF TABLES AND DIAGRAMS

ACKNOWLEDGEMENTS

Congress would like to thank the following contributors to our Centenary Conference on 'Ireland in the 21st Century' for participating in the Conference and for making their papers available:

NORBERT ALTMAN, Research Director, Institute of Social Research, Munich

ROBERT CORNELL, Deputy General Secretary, OECD

DEIRDRE CURTIN, Professor of Law of International Organisations, University of Utrecht

PHILIP FLYNN, President, Irish Congress of Trade Unions

JOHN KENNETH GALBRAITH, Harvard University

EAMONN HALL, Author of *The Electronic Age*, Company Solicitor, Telecom Éireann

MICHAEL HANSENNE, Director General, International Labour Organisation

LIM BOON HENG, General Secretary, Singapore National Trade Union Congress

NUALA KEHER, Adult Education Centre, University of Limerick

LISELOTTE KNUDSEN, Vice-President, Union of Commercial & Clerical Employees, Denmark

DAVID MCCONNELL, Professor of Genetics, Trinity College, Dublin

CHARLIE MCDONALD, AFL–CIO Committee on Evolution of Work

JOHN MONKS, General Secretary, British Trades Union Congress

BRIAN NANGLE, Executive Director, Munekata (Ireland) Ltd.

RORY O'DONNELL, Director, National Economic and Social Council

RUAIRI QUINN, TD, Minister for Enterprise and

Employment
PETER SUTHERLAND, Director General, GATT
FRIEDRICH VERZETNITSCH, President, European
Trade Union Confederation.

We would also like to thank the European Commission and
Power Supermarket Group for their generous support for this
publication.

We thank the organisations and publishers which
agreed to us using materials/charts from their publications:

OECD for material Copyright © OECD
International Labour Office Publications for materi-
al Copyright © International Labour Organisation,
Geneva
Simon and Schuster for an extract taken from *The
Work of Nations* by Robert Reich, published by
Simon & Schuster, London in 1992, © Robert Reich,
1992
EU for material Copyright © EU
NESC for material Copyright © NESC
FÁS for material Copyright © FÁS
Meitheal Mhuigheo/Galway VEC for material
Copyright © Meitheal Mhuigheo/Galway VEC.

We also thank the World Trade Organisation, Geneva and
the Central Statistics Office, Dublin, for help given with
statistical data; Eolas, Engineering Departments, Trinity
College, University College, Dublin, Limerick City University for information on new materials, and Nuala Brennan
for typing.

SERVING OUR CUSTOMERS

These are some of the 7,000 people in the Power Supermarkets Group committed to serving our customers. In close association with our Trading Partners, we take a special pride in the relationships we build with our customers. Serving them well is the key to success for all of us.